LOVE & GO

12 Powerful Truths for a Blessed Life

FRANK KELLY III

FOREWORD BY JON GORDON

Wall Street Journal Best-Selling Author of The Energy Bus and The Hard Hat

ISBN: 979-8-9942099-1-2
Library of Congress Control Number: 2025927832

Book design and layout by Jennifer Kozak, Thats Klutch, LLC.
Cover design by Jennifer Kozak

Publishing services provided by Gordon Publishing
GordonPublishing.com

First printing: 2026

Printed in the United States of America.

Frank Kelly III
c/o Kelly Benefits
1 Kelly Way
Sparks, MD 21152

LoveAndGo.com
FrankKellyIII.com

DEDICATION

I dedicate this book to my wife Gayle, our children—Frankie and his wife, Acacia; Stephen and his wife, Caroline; Jackie and JK—our grandchildren, Quin, Brooks, and Truett; any future grandchildren and great-grandchildren; and to all seekers of truth.

CONTENTS

PART ONE

LOVE

Chapter 1 - The Power of God's Word—The Bible

TRUTH #1:

The Bible is God's Word, and it is living, active,
and full of powerful truth that can bless your life and set you free
to be all that God created you to be.

1

Chapter 2 - The Power of Praise

TRUTH #2:

When you praise God, you express faith, invite Him into your life
situations, and lay a foundation to experience freedom and peace.

11

Chapter 3 - The Power of Prayer

TRUTH #3:

Prayer is simply communication with our Creator, God,
that has power to change our hearts, lives, and the world.

23

Chapter 4 - The Power of the Holy Spirit

TRUTH #4:

The key to supernatural living and fulfilling your
unique purpose in life is being plugged into God's power
by being filled with the Holy Spirit.

41

PART TWO

GO

FOREWORD

With two simple words, *Love* and *Go,* Frank Kelly conveys the most significant message we can live and share with the world. And with twelve powerful truths, he reveals how our choices and actions can lead to a blessed life.

It blew my mind that Frank captured and embodied two of the greatest teachings in all of Scripture—the Great Commandment and the Great Commission—in those two short but profound words.

As I looked at *Love & Go* on the cover and read the book, I kept shaking my head—in a good way. The brilliance, simplicity, and power of it leap off the pages of this life-changing book for all of us to see, live, and share.

Jesus told his disciples to *Love* and *Go.* Those two words would change their lives, the course of history, and the world. And I believe those two words will change your future, your life, and your world.

You don't have to wait to make an impact. You can *Love* and *Go* right now. You can *Love* and *Go* tomorrow and the next day. You can put these twelve powerful truths into practice and watch your life become a blessing to others. You can shine a light in the darkness of this world and make it a more loving, positive place.

I'm excited you are reading this book, because I know it will inspire you to love deeper, go further, rise higher, experience more joy, and live a blessed life.

Jon Gordon

Wall Street Journal Best-Selling Author of The Energy Bus and The Hard Hat

PREFACE

How did you end up with this book? Did a friend refer it or give it to you? Did you buy or download it online? Did you lose a bet and have to read it?

Regardless of how or why you picked it up, it is not in your hands at this time by accident.

In it, I share stories about my life, my family, and our business, but its true purpose is to share powerful truths that will encourage, strengthen, and bless your story, while ultimately honoring God and His story.

Part of my story that I hate to admit is that during my college years, I rarely read the books that were assigned. Instead, I often turned to *CliffsNotes*, which summarized the key points of those books. They saved me a lot of time while still allowing me to understand the main messages of the assigned books I didn't read.

Today, I love reading books, and it's from that love that I was inspired to write this one. My goal with this book is to share key, powerful truths that have blessed my life in a *CliffsNotes* kind of way, condensing decades of reading and learning into this consolidated, easy-to-read text.

This book is not structured like a novel where each chapter builds on the previous one. Instead, each chapter stands on its own, though you will see a common thread that ties them all together.

I encourage you to engage with it in unique ways. Feel free to write in it, highlight passages, earmark pages, jot down questions in the margins, and if possible, reflect on and later discuss the end-of-chapter questions with a friend or group of friends.

I would also encourage you to use the written prayer at the end of each chapter as a way to communicate your thoughts and feelings to God. Feel free to change the words to accurately reflect your heart and hopes regarding the chapter topic. And if you are comfortable, before you read each chapter, take a moment to open your hands and quietly ask God for wisdom to help you see what you need to see, hear what you need to hear, and learn what you need to learn.

No matter where you are in your personal faith journey or relationship with God, my hope is that this book leaves you intellectually and spiritually inspired in practical, relevant, and meaningful ways. May you find at least one gold nugget in each chapter that will bless your life for many years to come.

INTRODUCTION

In 2024, I celebrated two milestone birthdays in the same year. I was born on Valentine's Day, February 14, 1964, in Philadelphia, Pennsylvania, before my family moved to Baltimore, Maryland, when I was young. I experienced a second birth, really, a spiritual rebirth or awakening, twenty years later, in February 1984, on a lacrosse field in Ithaca, New York.

On February 14, 2024, my wife Gayle threw me a big "60/40 LOVE" birthday party, as she called it, to celebrate my sixtieth physical birthday and my fortieth spiritual birthday. She transformed our house into a mini "Little Italy" featuring the best dishes from our favorite restaurants in Baltimore's Little Italy and the surrounding area.

More than one hundred friends and family members filled our home for an unforgettable Valentine's Day dinner and birthday celebration. My main hope for the evening was to say "Thank you!" to everyone in attendance for the unique and positive ways they had blessed and influenced me.

During the party, I was roasted and toasted by a number of friends, a couple of my brothers, and even two of my sons. After everyone had some laughs—at my expense—I stood and expressed my love and gratitude for Gayle, our children and grandchildren, my extended family, everyone in attendance, and all who had poured encouragement and truth into my life over the years.

Leading up to this special Valentine's/birthday dinner, and even as I spoke and looked into the eyes of everyone at the party, I got a strong sense that I was supposed to record and share key powerful truths I had learned over my "60/40 journey" that had blessed my life, in hopes that these truths would bless them and many other people as well.

A theme for my life has become "Love & Go"—desiring each day to *love* God completely, *love* others compassionately, *love* myself correctly, and then *go* where God leads to share His love and truth in both word and deed.

Two of my "life words" are *faithful* and *intentional*. In recording these truths and writing this book, I wanted to be faithful and intentional to share some of the wisdom God has entrusted to me that might bless and empower you to more effectively "Love & Go" and fulfill your unique purpose and potential in life.

Somewhere along the way, I heard it said, "You will be the same person in five years as you are today, except for the people you meet and the books you read." I've found that to be true, and I am very grateful for the amazing people, inspiring books, and other sources of learning that God, in His grace, has brought into my life over the years.

The twelve powerful truths I share and expound on in this book were revealed to me through people I have met or words I have read, or listened to. For more than forty years, I have kept journals and written down notes and quotes from nearly every sermon or message I have heard.

While I have done my best to properly credit each author and source of learning, I am afraid I may fall short here. To every author, teacher, coach, and speaker who has shed light on the powerful truths I now share, I am indebted and thankful.

By nature, I am a collector and connector of friends, relationships, experiences, and truths. In this book, I share the very best of my collected "notes and quotes," stories, and experiences in a way that I hope connects and draws you closer to God and inspires you to *love* and *go* in unique and powerful ways.

PART ONE
LOVE

The Power of God's Word— The Bible

TRUTH #1:

The Bible is God's Word, and it is living, active, and full of powerful truth that can bless your life and set you free to be all that God created you to be.

"All Scripture is God-breathed and is useful for teaching, rebuking, correcting and training in righteousness, so that the servant of God may be thoroughly equipped for every good work."[1]

The Apostle Paul

Did you know the Bible is the No. 1 bestselling book in history? Have you ever questioned whether the Bible is really God's Word and filled with truth, or if it's just a collection of myths or illustrations to drive home various values or points? Have you ever wondered whether the Holy Scriptures are really that holy or even relevant to life today? I know I have!

It was during my junior year in college at Cornell University that I was invited to a Bible study for the first time. Six months earlier, in February of my sophomore year, I experienced a spiritual awakening in the middle of lacrosse practice, which opened me up to growing in my faith and learning more about having a relationship with God.

My friend Jeff, whom I had met two years earlier while playing on the freshman football team, told me about a fraternity/sorority Bible study that he and his roommate Gregg had started. It was held on Monday nights at their Sigma Chi fraternity house, and Jeff encouraged me to check it out.

Growing up, I had heard some scriptures from the Bible read out loud at church, but I had never really read or studied them for myself. To be honest, most of what I heard at church went in one ear and out the other as I daydreamed about sports, girls, and whatever else floated through my mind.

I showed up to that first Bible study a little late and very nervous. I carried the only Bible I owned. It was a pocket-sized version that my father had gifted me for Christmas when I was thirteen years old.

I had never read the Bible my dad had given me, but I had read the note he wrote inside:

Dear Frank,
The solutions to any problem are in this great book. Try to read a
chapter each day of your life and you will be happy. The words in this
book come directly from God thru His Holy Spirit to you.
Seek God first thru His son Jesus Christ in all areas of your life,
and you will be guaranteed success. Pray regularly, Frank, and always
remember how much I love you.
Dad

The experience of my first Bible study was both awkward and inspiring. Jeff welcomed the seven or eight of us who had gathered that night in the small fraternity bedroom and said, "Hey, everyone! Welcome to our fraternity/sorority Bible study. To start tonight, let's all turn in our Bibles to the book of Ephesians."

I froze inside, panicking. *"Ephesians? Oh my God, where is that?"*

I quietly turned to the girl seated next to me and whispered, "Can you please tell me where Ephesians is?"

"Oh, it's easy," she said. "Just remember: Go, Eat, Pop, Corn."

"What?" I replied.

"Galatians, Ephesians, Philippians, Colossians. Ephesians is right after Galatians," she explained.

"Uh, okay, thank you."

I never found one verse that Jeff and Gregg referenced that night. I faked my way through the Bible, and I never said a word. But I noticed everyone else was very excited about their faith and the Scriptures. They read and talked about every word of the verses as if the words were real, powerful, and true.

I couldn't find any verses the second week either. Frustrated, I called home and told my mom I was attending a Bible study. She was so excited that she bought me a Bible with big tabs sticking out the side with the names of each book in the Bible so I could flip right to the actual book, chapter, and verses Jeff and Gregg referenced.

That Bible was a lifesaver, and over time, something incredible began to happen. The words we read and discussed began to jump off the pages and really speak to me. These words were different from any other words, from any other book that I had ever read before. They seemed so relevant and alive. But as we read and discussed the Scriptures, I began to wonder in my mind: *Was the Bible really trustworthy, reliable, and true?*

IS THE BIBLE TRUSTWORTHY?

I quickly discovered that I was not the only one asking this question. I learned that over the years, a number of well-educated people had questioned and set out to disprove the reliability and trustworthiness of the Bible.

One man named Josh McDowell was determined to prove that the Bible was false and that Judaism and Christianity were man-made religions based on various myths and made-up stories. After years of exhaustive research and study, McDowell reached the exact opposite conclusion. He found overwhelming evidence that the Bible is supernaturally inspired, historically accurate, and trustworthy as a foundation for one's life.

In his book, *Evidence That Demands a Verdict*, McDowell points out that the Bible was written over 1,500 years by more than forty different authors, across three different continents (Asia, Africa, and Europe), and in three languages (Hebrew, Aramaic, and Greek). The authors came from every walk of life, including kings, peasants, philosophers, fishermen, poets, statesmen, scholars, and even a former tax collector. Some of the Bible was written during times of war, and some during times of peace. Some was written from the heights of joy, and others from the depths of sorrow and despair. Its subject matter includes hundreds of controversial topics, yet the biblical authors spoke with harmony and continuity from the first book, Genesis, to the last, Revelation.

McDowell notes, "The Bible has been read by more people and published in more languages than any other book in history. The Bible has been translated and paraphrased more than any book in existence. It has survived through persecution—at times in history it has been burned, banned, and outlawed, from the days of the Roman emperors to present-day Communist-dominated countries—and it has survived through much criticism."[2]

In his daily devotional, *Daily Hope,* bestselling author and pastor Rick Warren writes, "The fact that the Bible has only one theme is nothing short of a miracle. It'd be one thing if one person wrote the Bible. The Qur'an was written by one person, Muhammad. The Analects of Confucius were written by Confucius. The Bible, on the other hand, was written by forty different people, at every age and stage in life, on three continents. And they all wrote the same story: Jesus' story. Prophets and poets, princesses and kings, sailors and soldiers, all had the same story. From Genesis to Revelation, the Bible is all about God redeeming humanity, and Jesus is its star. Having a simple unified theme is one of the reasons we know that the Bible is God's Word."[3]

Warren also writes, "Another reason we can know the Bible is true and trustworthy is that it has hundreds of prophecies that have come true. The Bible contains more than 300 prophecies about Jesus alone—many written more than a thousand years before He was born. The Bible prophesied about when He'd be born, where He'd be born, and who He'd be born to. It would be impossible for someone to manipulate His birth to fulfill those prophesies. It also predicted how He would die, a thousand years before He died. A thousand years before Jesus died, King David described Jesus' death on the cross in one of the Psalms. He didn't use the word 'crucifixion' because no one knew that word then. Long before the Romans were even thinking about crucifying people, David described it..."[4]

As I continued to study God's Word and read authors like McDowell, Warren, and others, my doubts about the Bible subsided, and my questions found answers. I came to firmly believe the Bible is trustworthy and true.

I like how theologian Bernard Ramm explained the power of the Bible, "A thousand times over, the death knell of the Bible has been sounded, the funeral procession formed, the inscription cut on the tombstone, and committal read. But somehow the corpse never stays put. The Bible is still loved by millions, read by millions, and studied by millions."[5]

It's incredible to know the Bible is the most read book in history, the bestselling book in history, and the most translated book in history. There is no other book in all of literature like it.

What is Truth?

I believe one of the greatest questions ever asked that happens to be recorded in the Bible came from Pontius Pilate, the Roman-appointed governor of Judea who presided over the trial of Jesus Christ. He asked Jesus, "What is truth?"[6]

Many documents record the historical reality that both Pilate and Jesus lived and that, indeed, Pilate had Jesus publicly beaten and crucified. This was done to please the Jewish leaders of the day, who threatened to disrupt Pilate's reign if he didn't take action against Jesus.

Pilate did not see anything wrong or bad in Jesus, and his wife even warned him to "...have nothing to do with this righteous man..."[7] But Pilate knew the Jewish leaders could create chaos in the city of Jerusalem and make him look bad in the eyes of his boss, the Roman Emperor, Tiberius Julius Caesar Augustus. Pilate caved under the pressure and sentenced Jesus to death. Yet his question, "What is truth?" still lives on. We all need to be willing to ask that question.

Before Jesus' encounter with Pilate, He once said of Himself, "I am the way and the truth and the life. No one comes to the Father except through Me."[8]

Three days after Jesus' death and burial, history records that He rose from the dead–proving His words are true: He is *the way* to the Father, and He is indeed *the truth*.

A Strong Foundation

Before His death, Jesus also told a story, or parable, about two men.[9] One man built his house upon a rock—the solid rock of God's Word received and applied to his life. When the storms of life came, his house stood firm. Another man built his house on sand—on the ever-changing truths, fads, and ways of the world. When the storms of life came, his house collapsed.

Jesus' lesson still applies today, and when we build our lives on God's truth, we can stand firm. The challenge is to receive and embrace God's Word by reading or listening to it, studying it to understand its context, memorizing it, meditating on it, and applying it to our lives.

The Bible was not written to just inform us, but to transform us and serve as a rock-solid foundation upon which to build and live our lives.

Jesus said to those who believed Him, "If you hold to my teaching [my words], you are really my disciples [followers]. Then you will know the truth, and the truth will set you free."[10]

Since my college years, I have continued to learn and grow in my belief that the Bible is fully trustworthy, reliable, and represents God's truth for us. The Bible is God's Word, a love letter to the world and to each of us as people created in His image. It is a game plan from God on how to live skillfully— with wisdom—and a guide for living a happy, healthy, and holy life.

The Bible is an extraordinary compilation of scripture that must be read, studied, and understood in the proper context of when it was written, to whom it was written, and why it was written. The fact that I don't understand every part of it does not disqualify any of it as being untrue.

Mark Twain once said, "Most people are bothered by those passages of scripture they do not understand, but the passages that bother me are those I do understand."[11]

I can relate to that. Can you?

Inspired – Living – Light

The Bible even has incredible things to say about itself in reference to being authentic, accurate, and true.

In one of the Apostle Paul's letters to his young friend and mentee Timothy, he writes, "All Scripture is God-breathed [another translation says 'inspired'] and is useful for teaching, rebuking, correcting and training in righteousness, so that the servant of God may be thoroughly equipped for every good work."[12]

As a former student-athlete and now a husband, father, grandfather, and businessman, I love the idea of being taught, corrected, and trained. We all need accountability and direction to be fully equipped for every good work and to fulfill our God-given potential.

Scripture also tells us, "...the word of God is living and active, and sharper than any two-edged sword..."[13] The Bible is not a book of outdated or irrelevant stories meant to sit on a shelf or table in your home and be viewed as a religious relic. It is *alive* and can speak to the deepest parts of your heart, mind, and soul.

The Bible also describes itself as a "lamp" for my feet and a "light" for my path.[14] We live in a day and age where darkness seems to surround us. Temptation, confusion, chaos, and evil are lurking around every corner. Yet God's Word serves as a lamp or light to lead us safely through the darkness.

The prophet Isaiah wrote, "The grass withers and the flowers fall, but the word of our God endures forever."[15] And the Scriptures quote Jesus saying, "Heaven and earth will pass away, but my words will never pass away."[16]

God's Word is eternal; it will endure forever and never change, because truth never changes. If something was true thousands of years ago, it remains true today and will still be true thousands of years from now.

Despite the fact that we live in a day and age of moral relativism where many people claim there is no absolute truth—your truth is your truth, and my truth is my truth—we ultimately cannot change or alter truth. We can only choose to accept it or reject it.

Warren also notes in *Daily Hope* that, "[There is] one fundamental question in life that stands above all others. What will have final authority [or truth] in your life? Most authority [or truth] options fall into three categories: (1) your opinions, (2) the world's perspective and opinions, or (3) God's Word. There is only one authority [or truth] that's always reliable and will never lead you astray. We have to decide if we want to allow God's Word to shape our values and decisions or the opinions of others and the world. The challenge is for you and me to give God's Word final authority in our lives."[17]

I've come a long way since my first Bible study, and God has brought many teachings and books into my life to further confirm the Bible's reliability and trustworthiness.

The following chapters have many references to God's Word, which is ultimately about LOVE. I hope the truths shared within each chapter strengthen your faith and the very foundation of your life, leading you to greater freedom and joy through a growing personal relationship with the God who created you.

A key to effectively *love* and *go* is to build your life on a foundation of truth, and reading, studying, and applying God's Word, the Bible, is a great start.

SUGGESTED PRAYER

Dear God,

Thank You for the gift of Your Word, the Bible. Please help me read, understand, and apply it to my life. I realize that Your Word is living, active, and full of power. May it strengthen the foundation of my life and guide me to love and go, becoming all that You created me to be and do.

In Jesus' name. Amen.

CHAPTER 1

The Power of God's Word—The Bible

TRUTH #1:

**The Bible is God's Word, and it is living, active,
and full of powerful truth that can bless your life and set you free
to be all that God created you to be.**

QUESTIONS FOR REFLECTION

1. What are three things you learned about God's Word, the Bible, from reading this chapter?

2. Which scripture or quote resonated with you most? Why?

3. Have you ever participated in a Bible study with others? If yes, how has it impacted your relationship with God? If not, would you consider joining one?

4. Have you downloaded an app (e.g., the Bible App by YouVersion) on your smartphone to access the Bible easily at any time? If not, consider downloading one now.

5. Is there a Bible study guide or daily Scripture reading plan (i.e., devotional) that has blessed or encouraged you? If so, what is it, and what do you like about it?

6. Does the final authority or truth in your life come from (a) your opinions, (b) the world, or (c) God's Word? Why?

The Power of Praise

TRUTH #2:

When you praise God, you express faith, invite Him into your life situations, and lay a foundation to experience freedom and peace.

"God inhabits the praises of His people."[1]

King David

One of my favorite stories in the Bible comes from the book of Acts. It is about the Apostle Paul and his companion Silas, who were unjustly beaten and locked up in a dark, dingy prison cell for proclaiming God's love and truth. Paul and Silas had every reason to feel angry, frustrated, distraught, and depressed. Instead, they chose to praise the Lord with their songs and prayers.

Luke, who wrote the book of Acts, records the event:

> After they had been severely flogged, they were thrown into prison, and the jailer was commanded to guard them carefully. When he received these orders, he put them in the inner cell and fastened their feet in the stocks.
>
> About midnight Paul and Silas were praying and singing hymns [of praise] to God, and the other prisoners were listening to them. Suddenly there was such a violent earthquake that the foundations of the prison were shaken. At once all the prison doors flew open, and everyone's chains came loose. The jailer woke up, and when he saw the prison doors open, he drew his sword and was about to kill himself because he thought the prisoners had escaped. But Paul shouted, "Don't harm yourself! We are all here!"
>
> The jailer called for lights, rushed in and fell trembling before Paul and Silas. He then brought them out and asked, "Sirs, what

must I do to be saved?"

They replied, "Believe in the Lord Jesus, and you will be saved—you and your household." Then they spoke the word of the Lord to him and to all the others in his house. At that hour of the night the jailer took them and washed their wounds; then immediately he and all his household were baptized. The jailer brought them into his house and set a meal before them; he was filled with joy because he had come to believe in God—he and his whole household.[2]

In the midst of deep pain, darkness, and despair, Paul and Silas praised the Lord.

Amazing!

Through the power of praise, the Lord worked miracles by loosening the prisoners' chains and setting them free. Ultimately, He used the testimony of the "loosed chains" to draw others, even the Philippian jailer and his family, into a personal faith and relationship with Jesus Christ.

The Lord can do the same miraculous thing in our lives. He can bring freedom, joy, and peace when we choose to praise Him each moment of the day.

HEAD TO HEART

I started playing organized sports when I was eight years old. During my first year of football and baseball, I was somewhat tentative and average at best. I was farsighted and wore thick glasses that magnified my eyes. More often than not, I broke my frames and had tape on at least one corner of my glasses. Sometimes, I even had tape on both corners and across the bridge of my nose. After I chipped my front right tooth and my parents didn't have the money to fix it, I was quite the sight.

By middle school, I had a thick mop of dark, curly, 1970s-style hair, taped-up glasses, and a chipped smile, so you can imagine I received some serious ribbing. That teasing pushed me to develop a toughness, what I would describe as "an angry edge" or "a chip on my shoulder," which started fueling my intensity both on and off the field. That intensity drove me to become a pretty good athlete.

By eighth grade, I was one of the top local youth football players being recruited by two powerhouse Baltimore-area Catholic high schools—Calvert Hall and Loyola Blakefield. Calvert Hall's coach, Augie Miceli, offered me a $500 annual scholarship (half the tuition at the time), and that, coupled with the atmosphere and culture of their football program, led me to choose "The Hall!"

During my freshman year, Calvert Hall lacrosse coach Mike Thomas convinced several freshman football players and me to play lacrosse in the spring instead of baseball, even though I had little to no experience. From then on, all the wheels were in motion.

By my senior year, football and lacrosse had gone from being *games* to *gods* in my life. Despite having some success, I often felt frustrated because so much of my identity revolved around my performance on the field.

I was recruited during my senior year to play lacrosse and, in some cases, football too, at Virginia, Cornell, Harvard, Bucknell, Washington and Lee, and others. I received scholarships from Virginia and Washington and Lee, and I was accepted to Harvard, but I ultimately chose Cornell University. Cornell offered the best opportunity to play NCAA Division I lacrosse at the highest level while still playing football and, not to mention, getting a solid education.

By the time I got to Cornell, I was into drinking and partying as well. I didn't realize how tough it would be to be a two-sport athlete, good student, and party boy. And I didn't heed the wise counsel of the Athletic Director, who challenged us as incoming freshmen to prioritize our studies and athletic endeavors over the party scene. Unfortunately, I tried to do all three, which led to a lack of sleep and some frustrating injuries, among other things.

During my freshman year, I injured my foot on the last play of our final football practice. That injury led me to training and running with a limp, which would eventually lead to serious shin splints and, ultimately, stress fractures. This hampered my spring lacrosse season and lingered for the next year and a half.

To make matters worse, the lacrosse coaches who recruited me didn't seem to think I was as talented as I thought I was, and I got little to no playing time. My "gods" were crumbling, and I was frustrated, angry, and full of bitterness. The harder I pressed and tried to overcome these feelings, the worse things seemed to get.

During that dark time, God placed several people in my life who helped me consider a new way forward. My football teammate, Jeff Caliguire, and an All-American wrestler, Pete Shaifer, were both passionate about their Christian faith. Each of them spoke to me separately about the importance of having a personal relationship with God.

My parents, who had experienced a spiritual awakening a few years earlier, reminded me of this as well. My father would say, "Frankie, until your relationship with God, through His Son Jesus Christ, is your top priority, you will not have peace."

At that time, the concept of a personal relationship with God just didn't make sense to me. My parents' and friends' words went in one ear and out the other. I dismissed their advice, telling Jeff and Pete that I had *some religion*, I believed in God, and I even went to church sometimes. Several of my Cornell teammates and I occasionally attended the 5 p.m. service at Anabel Taylor Hall on Sundays, which we jokingly called the "hangover mass" because we, and many others, would often be hungover from the weekend activities.

Pete asked me one day, "Do you know the distance between religion and a relationship with God?"

"No, what is it?" I asked.

"Eighteen inches—from your head to your heart," he replied.

I had many pieces of the spiritual puzzle from my Irish Italian Catholic upbringing, but for some reason, I didn't understand how they all fit together, nor did I comprehend the idea of a personal relationship with God the Father, through His Son, Jesus Christ.

One day, during my sophomore year in February 1984, in the middle of lacrosse practice on Cornell's Schoellkopf Field in Ithaca, New York, it all came together in a painful, powerful, and real way.

Cornell's Hall of Fame coach, Richie Moran, had been pushing me hard during practice. During a particular line drill, in front of the entire team, Coach Moran had me go to the goal against one of our defenders. As I began my dodge, he knocked the ball out of my stick.

"Kelly, go again!" Coach Moran yelled.

I went again, and the defender stripped the ball from me a second time. This time, Coach Moran, louder and with a few expletives, yelled, "Kelly, go again!" For a third time, that defender took the ball away from me. Humiliated in front of my teammates, I was told by Coach Moran that I would never get on the field at Cornell. At that moment, all of my anger, fear, and frustration came to a head.

I went to the end of the drill line, and for the first time in my life, apart from any parental pressure or religious expectation, I stood on my own two feet, and with tears in my eyes, cried out to God. I whispered a simple, heartfelt prayer under my breath:

Lord, that is it! If I never play football or lacrosse again, I need You in my life. I have blown it many times, and I'm sorry. I want to prioritize a relationship with You and ask You, Jesus, to come into my heart and make me the person You desire me to be. I need Your help. Amen!

I did not see lightning or hear thunder, but something changed that day.

When I was fourteen years old, I went through the Sacrament of Confirmation at our family church and was confirmed in my *head*, but on that day on the lacrosse field, as a twenty-year-old sophomore in college, I was confirmed in my *heart*.

The symbols of Confirmation are a flame and a dove, which represent the Holy Spirit, or the third person of the Trinity. After my *head* confirmation, which was a family requirement, I received cards with money inside and pictures of an upside-down dove or tongues of fire on the outside, but I just didn't understand the concept of opening my heart and life to receive Jesus and the Holy Spirit.

But that day on the lacrosse field, God allowed me to be humbled. There, on my own, apart from any religious ceremony or ritual, I opened my heart and life to Jesus. Although I didn't realize it at the time, I believe the Holy Spirit came into me then as well, and I was reborn spiritually.

MY PRAISE STORY

When I got home that night after practice, I called my dad and shared my decision. He was excited for me. As we wrapped up our conversation, and before he prayed for me, he said:

> Frankie, the best and most practical advice I can give you is to praise the Lord every minute that you can. You don't need to be in church or with others to praise Him. Morning, noon, and night, in good times and bad, wherever you go, under your breath quietly, praise and thank the Lord. When you walk across the campus, during lacrosse practice, every spare moment you have, dedicate it to praising God. And this may not make sense, but especially praise Him when it appears that things are going badly. You don't need to praise Him *for* every situation, but you should try to praise Him *in* every situation.

Wow! What a concept—constant praise. The next day, as I walked across campus, I began to praise the Lord quietly in my mind. I praised and thanked Him that I could see, that I could walk, that I was at Cornell, and that I had family and friends. I praised Him for everything I could conceive.

There is a scripture that talks about God inhabiting the praises of His people.[3] So, I learned that by praising God in a situation, I was actually expressing faith (Who would give praise or thanks to someone or something that did not exist?) and inviting God to inhabit and come into my life situations.

At practice the next day, I was still between the third- and fourth-string midfield line. My shin splints and stress fractures still hurt, and Coach Moran was still all over me. He even grabbed my face mask and shook it as he yelled at me, trying to make me a better player. A lot was still wrong, but for the first time in a long time, I had peace—no anger, no frustration, no fear—just peace.

I praised the Lord under my breath throughout that practice, and I began to have a clear sense that God was setting me free. He was breaking the chains of negativity that had been controlling me.

Through my new relationship with God and the power of praise, I could experience what He wanted me to experience and be freed up to become the person He wanted me to be. I was learning that there was something supernatural and powerful about praising the Lord.

Regardless of life's circumstances, when we praise God, we are telling Him that we trust Him and believe He is who He claims to be.

God Wink

It was about three weeks after I began praising God, mainly under my breath throughout the day and during practice, that God chose to give lacrosse back to me in a miraculous way.

Late in the third quarter of our first game of the year at Adelphi University, which we were favored to win, we were down by five or six goals. Our first- and second-string faceoff guys were struggling, and we were getting beaten badly. Coach Moran even put in a player who didn't face off or play my position before he put me in, which in the past would have absolutely infuriated me.

Instead, I was standing on the sideline in the cold, windy rain, down with the other reserve players, quietly praising God under my breath, "I praise You for life and health and for the chance to be at Adelphi University with the Cornell team." That is when I heard my name being called.

"Kelly, you take the next faceoff!" barked Coach Moran.

My hands were frozen; I could barely feel my fingers and toes. I didn't even have time to take off my sweatpants as I ran onto the field.

Yet, I ended up having a big game. I won a bunch of faceoffs, scored a goal and an assist, and led our team back to a near victory.

We lost the game 13-12, but in the locker room after the game, my teammates were saying, "Frankie, you were on fire and totally possessed out there!"

On the bus ride back to Ithaca, Coach Moran came over to me and said, "Hey Kelly, that was one of the greatest games I have ever seen anyone play coming off the bench. Great job!" At that moment, I felt like God winked at me.

I had no deal with God. No quid pro quo. I didn't tell Him three weeks earlier on the turf at Schoellkopf Field that I would give Him my life if He would give lacrosse back to me. I thought my lacrosse career was over, and I had peace with that—His peace that surpasses understanding. For whatever reason, God chose to bless me that day. And although I didn't realize it at the time, when my teammates said I played like I was possessed, I now believe it was God Himself, in the form of the Holy Spirit, who played through me that day.

Little did I know what God had planned for me on the lacrosse field in the future. I ended up starting every game for the next three years, ultimately becoming a captain and receiving some nice honors and recognition. I would go on to play professionally and continue playing and coaching for many years after college. I would even be involved in helping start and lead a ministry to help reach, serve, and bless the lacrosse community around the world.

WHY PRAISE?

Praising God doesn't always mean things will go your way, but it does mean you will have His grace, power, and blessing to:

- Recognize God for who He is—all-powerful, all-knowing, and everywhere present.

- Invite God into your situations, as His Word reminds us that He inhabits, indwells, and moves in and through the praises of His people.

- Experience the supernatural peace and freedom that only He can provide.

The Apostle Paul wrote to the young church in Thessalonica (which is Greece's second-largest city today) and encouraged them to, "Rejoice always, pray continually, give thanks in all circumstances; for this is God's will for you in Christ Jesus."[4]

Paul modeled the power of praise and reminded us that it's God's will for us to continually give Him praise and thanks. The powerful truth that God inhabits the praises of His people has changed my life.

Praise is an expression of LOVE, affirming God's love for us and our love for Him.

To *love* and *go* with greater joy and peace, praise Him. It will bless you, I promise. And more importantly, He promises.

SUGGESTED PRAYER

Dear God,

Help me learn to praise You minute by minute and hour by hour of each day. Thank You for Your promise that You inhabit the praises of Your people and bring freedom, joy, and peace when and where we praise You. In Jesus' name. Amen.

CHAPTER 2

The Power of Praise

TRUTH #2:

When you praise God, you express faith, invite Him into your life situations, and lay a foundation to experience freedom and peace.

QUESTIONS FOR REFLECTION

1. What stands out to you about the story of Paul and Silas in the prison in Acts 16:23-34?

2. How do you feel about the idea of praising God anytime and anywhere, especially during challenging times?

3. Do you believe that "God inhabits the praises of His people"? What does this scripture mean to you?

4. Are there areas in your life where you are seeking freedom or peace right now? Describe them.

5. What strikes you most from the verse, "Rejoice always, pray continually, give thanks in all circumstances, for this is God's will for you in Christ Jesus."?

6. Did any parts of my faith story—developing a personal relationship with God or learning to praise—resonate with you? Where are you in your personal faith journey? Have you opened your heart and life to receive Jesus and the Holy Spirit?

The Power of Prayer

TRUTH #3:

Prayer is simply communication with our Creator, God, that has power to change our hearts, lives, and the world.

"The prayer of a righteous person is powerful and effective."[1]

*James**

As I began to grow in my personal relationship with God, through the small group Bible study at the Sigma Chi fraternity, the leaders, Jeff and Gregg, challenged me and others to do more than just read and reflect on God's Word. They encouraged us to talk with God daily and to take time to listen to Him as well. In other words, to pray. They explained that, like any other relationship, a relationship with God requires two-way communication to grow closer together.

I had recently discovered the power of praise, which itself is a form of prayer. However, there was so much more I needed to learn about prayer and communicating with God.

I grew up in a faith tradition where prayer was mostly something you did before a meal or once a week at church. The prayers at church were usually read aloud and recited word for word, often in Old English. Some prayers were recited over and over, as if saying the words of the prayer repeatedly worked like rubbing a lucky rabbit's foot.

After my parents experienced a spiritual awakening in the mid-1970s, they began praying out loud, and their prayers were easy to understand and felt like direct conversations with God. Similarly, when Jeff and Gregg opened and closed each week's fraternity/sorority Bible study, they prayed

---

* Some theologians refer to the author of the book of James in the Bible as "James the Just" and others refer to him as James, the half-brother or cousin of Jesus.

out loud, talking to God like He was someone they actually knew. No flowery words or formal recitations, just straightforward conversation.

Wow! I thought. I never knew you could talk to God like that. I soon discovered that even Jesus' closest followers had a lot to learn about prayer. At one point, they turned to Jesus and said, "Lord, teach us to pray..."[2]

Clearly, they had questions about prayer, just like I did—and maybe you do too.

THE LORD'S PRAYER

When asked for help with prayer, Jesus responded to His disciples with what has become known as "The Lord's Prayer" or "The Our Father." He told them that when you pray, say:

Our Father, who art in heaven, hallowed be thy Name.
Thy kingdom come, thy will be done, on earth as it is in heaven.
Give us this day our daily bread.
And forgive us our trespasses, as we forgive those who trespass against us.
And lead us not into temptation, but deliver us from evil.
For thine is the kingdom, and the power, and the glory, for ever and ever.
Amen.[3]

The Lord's Prayer is recorded in two of the four Gospels, which are the life accounts of Jesus. The version above comes from the Gospel of Matthew, while there is a shorter version with slightly different wording in the Gospel of Luke. Although I appreciate when we all say the Lord's Prayer together in church, or in a sports locker room before or after a game, I don't think Jesus wanted His followers to just repeat the same exact words over and over again. Instead, both versions of The Lord's Prayer offer a model for prayer that shares the same key elements or components to guide our prayers.

A-C-T-S

Many years ago, I learned an acronym called A-C-T-S that has helped me remember the key elements of The Lord's Prayer and other instructions on prayer found in the Bible: **A**doration, **C**onfession, **T**hanksgiving, and **S**upplication.

Adoration

Adoration is acknowledging the greatness and glory of God, and a wise way to start our prayers.

As my good friends Father Michael White and Tom Corcoran explain in their book *Rebuilt Faith*, "Jesus wasn't only teaching a specific prayer; He was teaching how to pray."[4]

They note that, "In adoration . . . we begin by praising God and recognizing his goodness and greatness and holiness, and . . . we recognize our proper place in the universe before the God who created it. He is the Creator. We are the created. He is the Savior. We are the saved. He is the Sanctifier. We are the sanctified . . . we did not choose God; God chose us. We are reminded that when we 'hallow,' or worship, adore, and prioritize our heavenly Father's name, his kingdom, and his perfect will to be done, we acknowledge that . . . our lives and very existence overflow from God's loving goodness. For this reason, Jesus teaches us to begin our prayer with adoration and worship."

Confession

After adoration, it is good to focus on confession, where we admit, acknowledge, and confess our sins about when we have messed up and fallen short of God's best.

The Lord's Prayer, as recorded in Luke, encourages us to pray, "Forgive us our trespasses [or sins], as we forgive those who have trespassed [or sinned] against us."[5]

The Scriptures also remind us that we "all have sinned and fall short of the glory of God,"[6] and, "the wages [or result] of sin is death [or spiritual separation from God], but the gift of God is eternal life in Christ Jesus our Lord."[7]

God's Word calls us to "Confess your sins . . . and pray for each other so that you may be healed," and that "The prayer of a righteous [forgiven] person is powerful and effective."[8]

We are also assured, "If we confess our sins, He [God] is faithful and just and will forgive us our sins and purify us from all unrighteousness."[9]

God wants His best for us, so He tells us we can come directly to Him, at any time, from anywhere, about anything. This includes asking for our sins or trespasses to be forgiven. He promises to cleanse and forgive us if we confess our sins to Him. He also reminds us about the healing that comes when we confess our sins to another person, like a priest, counselor, or friend.

God also knows and reminds us how important it is for us to forgive the sins and debts of those who have wronged us. His Word says, "if you forgive other people when they sin against you, your heavenly Father will also forgive you. But if you do not forgive others their sins, your Father will not forgive your sins."[10]

Wow! That is a powerful statement.

It is so easy to harbor resentments and anger toward those who have offended, hurt, or sinned against us. However, holding onto such bitterness and resentment is harmful; it is like swallowing poison and hoping it kills the person who hurt you.

I once heard author Ney Bailey quote theologian Lewis B. Smedes and say, "To forgive is to set the prisoner free, only to discover that the prisoner was you." True freedom, healing, and peace come from forgiveness.

Thanksgiving

Thanksgiving is my favorite kind of prayer. Although it is not directly highlighted in The Lord's Prayer, God's Word speaks a great deal about it. We have so much to be thankful for, including God's love, grace, mercy, and blessings in our lives.

In the Old Testament, there are many psalms of thanksgiving, and a favorite of mine says, "Give thanks to the Lord, for He is good. His love endures forever."[11]

One of the few scriptures that says, "This is God's will for you..." comes from a letter the Apostle Paul wrote to the early church in Thessalonica. He wrote, "Rejoice always, pray continually, give thanks in all circumstances, for this is God's will for you in Christ Jesus."[12] From this verse, we can be certain about three things that are God's will for us: "rejoice always," "pray continually," and "give thanks" in all circumstances. It's worth noting that Paul doesn't say to give thanks *for* all circumstances, but *in* all circumstances.

Prayers of thanksgiving are undoubtedly God's will!

Supplication

Prayers of supplication or petition involve asking God for something for others or yourself.

The Apostle Paul wrote about prayers of supplication to the early church in Philippi (located in modern-day Greece) when he said, "Do not be anxious about anything, but in every situation, by prayer and petition, with thanksgiving, present your requests to God. And the peace of God, which transcends all understanding, will guard your hearts and minds in Christ Jesus."[13]

Prayers of supplication, when paired with thanksgiving, lead to peace!

The Lord's Prayer clearly calls for prayers of supplication, as Jesus teaches His followers to pray for "our daily bread," or our daily physical, mental, emotional, and spiritual needs to be met. God is our provider, and we are wise to seek His provision and then thank Him for it once it comes.

The Lord's Prayer finishes with a request, "And lead us not into temptation, but deliver us from evil."[14] The Scriptures make it clear that we are in a spiritual battle, with a spiritual enemy, who wants to keep us from experiencing God's best and a personal, real, exciting relationship with Him.

Jesus wants us to have the joy of answered prayer. In the Gospel of John, He says, "Until now you have not asked for anything in my name. Ask and you will receive, and your joy will be complete."[15]

When we come to God in supplication, we should do so with confidence, humility, and perseverance, bringing specific requests for ourselves and on behalf of others. Prayer invites God into our problems and issues that may be bigger than us, but are definitely not bigger than Him.

At times, we may feel like God isn't listening or answering our prayers, or at least not in the way we hope. Rick Warren reminds us, "God loves us too much to give us everything we ask for in prayer. So, when God says 'no,' we've got three options: we can resist it, resent it, or rest and relax in it."[16]

God answers all our prayers with either "yes," "no," or "wait."

One of my personal prayers is that I would rest, relax, and trust in the Lord, whose ways are so much higher than my ways, and whose thoughts are so much higher than my thoughts.[17] This is easier said than done, but God promises to help us if we ask.

We learn from God's Word that we shouldn't be bashful about making requests. Jesus told His disciples "that they should always pray and not give up."[18]

Perseverance and prayer are consistent themes in Scripture. White and Corcoran note that, "Perseverance and prayer works. It always works, even if we don't get the answers we hoped for or according to the timeline we get. As we keep praying, God keeps working on purifying our hearts and building our character."

LISTENING

Another key element to growing in a vibrant relationship with anyone—and especially in communication with God—is listening. God can speak to us through the Bible, other people, circumstances, and what His Word describes as "a still, small voice," or "a gentle whisper."[19]

The prophet Elijah faced significant challenges when he cried out to God for discernment. God instructed him to go and stand on the mountain and wait for the Lord.[20] There, in the silence, Elijah waited, longing to hear God's voice. Suddenly, a mighty wind tore through the mountains and shattered the rocks, but the Lord was not in the wind. Then came an earthquake, but the Lord was not in the earthquake. Then came a fire, yet the Lord was not in the fire. Finally, there came "a gentle whisper" (or "a still, small voice"), and it was then that Elijah heard the voice of the Lord offering him encouragement and clear direction to move forward.

One of the keys to hearing God's voice and growing in a deeper relationship with Him is regularly finding a place of silence and solitude. How can you or I hear that "still, small voice" or "gentle whisper" if we are always surrounded by people or in loud places?

I am an extrovert who feels energized by being around others and engaging in social settings, so seeking solitude and silence does not come naturally to me. Yet, in God's Word, we read, "Very early in the morning, while it was still dark, Jesus got up, left the house and went off to a solitary place, where he prayed."[21]

To hear God's whisper, we sometimes need to get alone with Him and sit quietly in His presence. Jesus even invited His disciples to "Come with me by yourselves to a quiet place..."[22]

Over the years, as I have worked on getting better at listening to God and not just doing all the talking, I have found it to be a real challenge at times.

I can relate to the words of Henri Nouwen, a Dutch Catholic priest, who once wrote:

> In solitude, I get rid of my scaffolding, no friends to talk with, no telephone calls to make, no meetings to attend, no music to entertain, no books to distract, just me—naked, vulnerable, weak, sinful, deprived, broken—nothing! It is this nothingness that I have to face in my solitude, a nothingness so dreadful that everything in me wants to run to my friends, my work, and my distractions so that I forget my nothingness and make myself believe I am worth something. But that is not all. As soon as I decide to stay in my solitude [and silence], confusing ideas jump around in my mind, like monkeys in a banana tree.[23]

Can you relate too?

Write for My Soul

Whenever I seek quiet time alone with God to pray and listen, my thoughts often race in many directions. Those "monkeys" jump around in my mind, just like they do in a banana tree. To settle my mind and better connect with God, I have found two things to be most helpful.

First, I need to find a place where distractions are limited and where I can slowly disconnect from the noise and craziness of life. When time, flexibility, and resources allow, I love sitting alone on a beach, gazing out at the ocean. For some reason, I can sit there for hours, enjoying God's grandeur and communicating with Him.

More often than not, however, I retreat to a room in our home that I call "my prayer closet." We had this simple, small space built over twenty-five years ago when we moved into our house. I keep all my faith-based books there for quiet reading. I even placed a bird feeder outside the window so I can reflect on God's creation while reading His Word, praying, and listening for His voice and guidance.

The second key to quieting the "monkeys" in my mind has been the practice of journaling. Wherever I am—even on the beach—I find it hard to be still. When I do sit down alone, my thoughts often race, and I easily get distracted. Journaling, or writing out my prayers, is a discipline that has helped me slow down, settle my heart, and focus my mind, better accepting the Lord's challenge to "Be still, and know that I am God."[24]

I've kept a journal since my junior year of college. Over forty years, the journals I use have evolved into a simple spiral-bound notebook with three sections of college-ruled paper, protected in a pleather (fake leather) case—nothing flashy.

For me, journaling is primarily about writing letters to God. I mainly write thank-you notes, and sometimes lists, but I often include the elements of the A-C-T-S prayer.

In the first section of my journal, I usually start at the top of a fresh page by writing, "Dear God," followed by expressions of adoration. I then take time to acknowledge and confess my sins of omission—things I didn't do but should have—and commission—things I did but shouldn't have said, done, or thought. I write whatever God brings to my heart and mind, knowing that if I confess my sin, God is faithful and just to cleanse me.[25]

After confession (which I usually write in an abbreviated short-hand type of script so no one could decipher it—God knows my heart, so my written words don't matter that much to Him), I shift my focus to thanking God for specific blessings and lifting up specific prayer requests or supplications.

I often end by writing the letter "L" on the bottom of the page as a reminder to listen. I then try to pause and wait to hear God's voice or leading.

Most days, I do not hear anything profound or specific; instead, I reflect on my Bible reading for the day.

Journaling, which I usually do a couple of times a week, allows me to better concentrate and hear God's whispers when He speaks them.

In his book *Experiencing God*, Henry Blackaby wrote, "If the God of the universe tells you something or teaches you something, you should definitely write it down."[26]

In the back two sections of my journal notebook, I record notes, reflections from Scripture, and impressions from church on Sundays or from Bible studies. Whenever I hear someone speak and share truth, I have my journal and a pen ready to record whatever speaks to me.

I have heard it said that "a dull pencil is better than a sharp mind," and that has been very true for me, especially when you consider that some learning models show we forget 95 percent of what we hear within seventy-two hours.

The blessing from a journal lasts far beyond daily communication with God. It provides a record to reflect on past prayers and an opportunity to see God's goodness and faithfulness in my life—both in the little things that felt important at the time and in the big things that have lifelong impacts. I am blessed to have forty years of written prayers and "notes and quotes" that continue to remind me of God's love and truth to this day.

My friends Jeff and Mindy Caliguire wrote a booklet about journaling titled *Write for Your Soul*. In it, they say, "A journal can act as an 'album' of thoughts and experiences, so by consciously recording some of our prayers and history, our past becomes more 'user-friendly' to us ourselves, and more accessible to future generations."[27]

My dozens of filled journals from over the decades have certainly been that to me, and I hope they will be a blessing to my family and others in the future. It is true that "we remember what we record."

POPCORN PRAYER

For decades, my three brothers and I have worked together in our family business. And for years, we have worked with a spiritual leadership coach/

advisor who meets with us monthly to help prioritize and live out our mission of being "...an organization committed to the pursuit of excellence, in an effort to bring honor and glory to God..." and our values of integrity, excellence, respect, humility, and generosity. It has been hard work, but we have each continued to grow and mature in our relationships with God and each other.

In 2014, our spiritual leadership coach/advisor encouraged each of us to consider individually attending an intensive, five-day, faith-based leadership retreat through an organization called His High Places. As the oldest brother and CEO of Kelly Benefits, I agreed to go first.

I decided to attend the five-day retreat alone to receive feedback, counsel, and direction. The following week, I chose to attend the same five-day retreat again (I'm a slow learner), this time with my wife Gayle, so she could experience it as well. It was a powerful time of learning and growth, both in our personal relationships with God and in our relationship with each other.

One of the practical applications we took away was the idea of practicing "popcorn prayer" together each day. In the past, we had prayed together on occasion, and definitely before meals or special events, but daily "popcorn prayer" became a simple and meaningful way to regularly pray for each other, our family, and the needs of others.

We were challenged to start each morning, even while still in bed, to go back and forth with short, simple praises, thanks, and prayers to God. To this day, we still practice popcorn prayer together almost every morning.

I often start by praying aloud something like, "Thank you, Lord, for this day and the gifts of life and health." Then Gayle might say, "Lord, You are so amazing. Thank you for the blessing of our family." After a few short, simple "popcorn praises," I might share a need, saying, "I have a need today for [blank]," and Gayle would then pray for my request. Then she might share, "I would like prayer for [blank]," and I would offer a brief prayer of blessing for her.

We continue going back and forth with simple but meaningful "popcorn prayers" for upcoming events, specific family concerns, and others in our sphere of influence. On days when I am up and out very early, I will often call

Gayle later, and we will do our "popcorn prayer" over the phone.

I have heard some interesting statistics about marriage and prayer that say while 50 percent of first marriages end in divorce, and 78 percent of second marriages end in divorce, less than 1 percent of couples who pray together daily end their marriages. I guess the old saying, "Families who pray together, stay together," is true!

Popcorn prayer can also bless groups and teams. Over the years, I have been involved with the Fellowship of Christian Athletes (FCA) and have coached many FCA Lacrosse teams. One of my favorite things to do with our players (and sometimes their parents too) after a game—win or lose—is huddle up and offer quick, short "popcorn prayers" of praise, thanksgiving, and supplication.

It is a joy to hear nine- and ten-year-old boys, or seventeen- and eighteen-year-old young men, and even parents, pray out loud, sometimes for the first time. Prayers like, "Thank you, Lord, for the game of lacrosse," "Thank you, God, for these amazing fields," "Thank you, Jesus, for our opponents and the referees who help us compete at a high level," "Thank you, Lord, for my parents who brought me to this game," or "Dear God, please heal Joey and his twisted ankle."

Pop, pop, pop—all it takes is simple prayers from the heart that bless and honor God to be reminded that prayer is simply communication with our Creator.

PRAYING SCRIPTURE

Over the years, Gayle and I have also learned the importance of praying Scripture over our children and grandchildren. Sometimes, we don't fully understand or know their real, deep, personal needs, so both individually and together, we will pray specific Bible verses over them.

When I am with my children or grandchildren, I often place my hand on their heads or shoulders and pray a specific scripture or God's blessing over them. Sometimes, I do this silently in my heart and mind, and other times, I do it out loud.

Did you know there are more than 7,000 promises in the Bible? A great way to start prayer is by reading, believing, and praying those promises. When we're unsure of what to say, we can use God's own words to guide our prayers.

One of my favorite scriptures to recite or pray is the blessing recorded by Moses in the book of Numbers, "The Lord bless you and keep you; the Lord make his face shine on you and be gracious to you; the Lord turn his face toward you and give you peace."[28]

Gayle's favorite scripture to pray comes from the book of Proverbs: "May love and faithfulness never leave you, may they be bound around your neck, and written on the tablet of your heart, so that you might win favor and a good name in the sight of God and man."[29]

Together, we often pray that God would bless our children and grandchildren and allow them, as Jesus did as a young boy, to grow "in wisdom and stature, and in favor with God and man."[30]

It is a great privilege and opportunity to pray for God's favor, blessing, and protection over our children, daughters-in-law, and grandchildren. We ask God to surround each member of our family with His angels[31] and His Spirit, keeping each from evil, injury, illness, or harm. We pray for God to bless and protect each person mentally, emotionally, physically, and spiritually. We often also ask God to bless our family and friends with the fruit of His Spirit, including His supernatural "love, joy, peace, patience, kindness, goodness, faithfulness, gentleness, and self-control."[32]

Prayer—this open, two-way communication with God, the Creator of the universe and all of life—is truly a blessing and privilege.

DESPERATION PRAYERS

The world champion boxer Mike Tyson once said about his preparation for a fight, "Everyone has a plan until they get punched in the mouth." Even with a "prayer plan," life can sometimes bring circumstances that feel like "a punch in the mouth" or a "kick in the gut," and our prayers can become more desperate and intense. An unexpected health crisis, a business challenge, or a relationship or family breakdown can literally bring us to our knees.

I can clearly remember the years of Gayle and my fertility challenges, as well as three different occasions over the last forty years when unforeseen circumstances confronted our business and nearly took us under. I also remember walking with our daughter through mental health challenges with anxiety, depression, and chronic fatigue.

I've heard it said, "In life you are either facing a significant challenge, coming out of a significant challenge, or entering a significant challenge."

Jesus said, "In this world you will have trouble."[33]

Some think God is too busy for us and our little problems, challenges, or prayers—after all, He is running the universe. In reality, we may get too busy for God, but He's never too busy for us.

Jesus said, "Are not five sparrows sold for two copper coins? And not one of them is forgotten before God. But the very hairs of your head are all numbered. Do not fear therefore; you are of more value than many sparrows."[34]

God even knows how many hairs are on our heads (which, unfortunately for me, is a shrinking number—but of course, God already knows that!). He is always more than willing to hear and respond to all of our prayers. Rick Warren writes, "An infinite God can be interested in an infinite number of things—at all the same time."[35]

In our times of pain, worry, fear, and desperation, we can cry out to God and communicate our concerns openly. All communication with God, even if it's loud, intense, and full of pain, is prayer. He can handle it and, more importantly, He welcomes our honest feelings and concerns.

As many Christians have said, "The shortest of all prayers in times of greatest need is simply, 'Help!'"

PRAYER CIRCLES

It was during the COVID-19 pandemic in early 2021 that a couple of Baltimore business leaders and I decided to pull together a group of business executives to meet once a month to pray for our city.

It was a very stressful time, with many businesses in Baltimore (and across the country) shutting down, while others tried to operate with employees working from home. We formed a group of twelve highly respected business leaders, including CEOs from some of Baltimore's largest employers, and we committed to connecting on the second Monday of each month for one hour from 7-8 a.m. using a relatively new technology called Zoom.

While most of us were active members of various nonprofit boards serving at-risk residents in Baltimore, none of us were meeting regularly with others to pray for our city. We were challenged by three scriptures from God's Word to commit to this time of prayer together.

The first was from the Apostle Paul's letter to the early church in Ephesus: "For our struggle is not against flesh and blood, but against the rulers, against the authorities, against the powers of this dark world and against the spiritual forces of evil in the heavenly realms."[36]

We could all see and sense a spiritual battle raging in our city and agreed that the best way to fight and win that battle was prayer.

The next scripture that inspired us was from the Gospel of Matthew, when Jesus was in the Garden of Gethsemane in Jerusalem. He went there to pray with a small group of His closest followers before He was betrayed and ultimately sentenced to death. Multiple times, He separated from them to pray, and each time He returned, His disciples were asleep. Jesus said to them, "...So, could you not watch with me one hour? Watch and pray..."[37]

We acknowledged that, at times, we had been spiritually blind and asleep to the needs of our city, so we agreed to "watch and pray" for Baltimore.

The third verse came from the book of James in the Bible, which says, "The prayer of a righteous person is powerful and effective."[38] None of us was righteous on our own, but through our faith in Jesus, we each were made clean and, thus, righteous. By God's grace, we believed our prayers together would be powerful, effective, and transformative.

Most of us were not clergy or "paid to pray," nor did we consider ourselves prayer warriors. Probably half of the group had never even prayed out loud before, other than reciting prayers at church.

We were humble learners who agreed to reflect on God's Word and its teachings about prayer, share our personal faith stories, and pray for each of the seven spheres of influence in our city and most cultures: business; government; education; the arts; sports, media, and entertainment; faith leaders and families.

After our first year, we welcomed six additional business leaders into our circle. We continued meeting via Zoom twice a quarter and gathered in person once a quarter at various offices throughout Baltimore. We chose mainly "high places" with views overlooking the city and, whenever possible, prayed through the windows facing south, then east, north, and west.

After our second year of praying together monthly, we decided to host a Prayer Breakfast at The Center Club in downtown Baltimore, hoping fifty to one hundred other leaders might join us. We intentionally chose not to announce or promote it publicly or on social media, but we agreed to invite other business and community leaders as the Spirit led. The speakers would be members of our prayer circle, and we did not include any politicians or pastors, as we did not want to draw any attention to political parties or denominational differences.

More than a hundred people RSVP'd to attend the breakfast, and more than 200 people showed up. The staff at The Center Club did an amazing job, rolling out additional tables and chairs to accommodate everyone.

At the end of breakfast, before closing in prayer, I asked attendees to fill out a card placed at each seat, indicating if they were interested in joining a prayer circle or possibly helping lead one. More than one hundred people expressed interest in joining a prayer circle, and more than twenty-five noted they would be willing to help lead one in one of the seven spheres of influence.

Today, our original Baltimore Business Leaders Prayer Circle includes twenty-four participants, and there are now fourteen additional prayer circles meeting regularly to pray for the different spheres of influence in our city.

By God's grace, we have witnessed and experienced several positive developments and trends in Baltimore since we began praying. Murder and crime rates are down by more than 50 percent, and school testing results have improved significantly. Each of us, as prayer circle members, has grown in our personal relationship with God, our understanding and appreciation of His Word, and our love for one another and our city.

Jesus said, "For where two or three gather in my name, there am I with them."[39]

We have definitely experienced the presence of Jesus in our prayer circles. Our hope is that one day there will be dozens, and maybe hundreds, of prayer circles in our city and state.

White and Corcoran have it right: "Prayer has the power to change hearts, to change lives, and to change the world. Prayer has the power to change your world, because when you pray, you are inviting the almighty maker of heaven and earth into your life."

The challenge to *love* and *go*, both alone and with others, is to tap into the power of prayer. Doing so will significantly impact your LOVE relationship with God, your family, and so many others within your community and around the world.

SUGGESTED PRAYER

Dear God,
Thank You for wanting a personal, real, intimate relationship with me.
Please help me grow in my prayer life and communication with You.
Teach me to love and go while better listening and hearing what You
want to say and communicate to me. Thank You that prayer is real and
has the power to change my heart, my circumstances, and the lives of
others in my family, community, and around the world.
In Jesus' name. Amen.

The Power of Prayer

TRUTH #3:

**Prayer is simply communication with our Creator, God,
that has power to change our hearts, lives, and the world.**

QUESTIONS FOR REFLECTION

1. When reading The Lord's Prayer in Matthew 6 or Luke 11, what words or phrases stand out to you?

2. From the acronym A-C-T-S, which type of prayer resonates with you the most—Adoration, Confession, Thanksgiving, or Supplication? Why?

3. Which scriptures or quotes in this chapter spoke to you the most? Why?

4. What are your thoughts on "Popcorn Prayer?"

5. Have you ever journaled your prayers or used some other method to quiet your mind and guide your communication with God? How has that experience worked for you?

6. Do you have a particular time or place you like to pray? If so, when and where?

CHAPTER 4

The Power of the Holy Spirit

TRUTH #4:

**The key to supernatural living and fulfilling your
unique purpose in life is being plugged into God's power
by being filled with the Holy Spirit.**

*"But you will receive power when the Holy Spirit comes on you;
and you will be my witnesses in Jerusalem, and in all Judea
and Samaria, and to the ends of the earth."*[1]

Jesus

Have you ever checked into an old hotel or spent the night at someone's house, and you needed to find an outlet or power source to charge your phone, but you couldn't find one? A smartphone with no power is useless. Imagine an unplugged TV or refrigerator; both are worthless. And a lamp cannot produce light and has no real value if it's not plugged into a power source.

For the first twenty years of my life, I was completely unaware that there was a supernatural power source made available to us from God that could help us become all that He created us to be.

I would learn that God's supernatural power source is not just a positive mental attitude, self-help psychology, or "pull yourself up by your bootstraps" thinking. This power source—the Holy Spirit—can actually help us live with purpose, navigate life's challenges, and bear the fruit of love, joy, peace, patience, kindness, goodness, faithfulness, gentleness, and self-control[2] while we do it.

After Jesus' life, death on a cross, burial, and resurrection from the dead,

He appeared more than a dozen times to His followers over the next forty days. The last thing Jesus said to them before He ascended into heaven was, "You will receive power when the Holy Spirit comes on you; and you will be my witnesses..."[3]

When Jesus ascended, it would be ten more days before the Holy Spirit would come as "tongues of fire"[4] and rest upon, come into, and fill these followers of Jesus. They were transformed by the power of the Holy Spirit and went from scared, timid believers hiding in their houses to bold, passionate witnesses who shared Jesus' love, grace, truth, and teachings.

It's exciting to know that when we open our hearts and invite Jesus into our lives, the same power that raised Jesus from the dead and fell upon His first followers is available to us every minute of every day. Regardless of the challenges we are facing, if we humble ourselves, fully surrender our lives, and plug into the Holy Spirit, His power can live and flow in and through us.

MY HOLY SPIRIT STORY

Growing up, I had heard about the Holy Spirit. I even made the sign of the cross—*In the name of the Father, and the Son, and the Holy Spirit*—on my forehead, then my chest, then across my shoulders whenever I went to church.

As I shared earlier in the "Power of Praise" chapter, I went through the Sacrament of Confirmation at our family church when I was fourteen years old. Through that process, I was supposed to learn about the Holy Spirit and then, as an emerging adult, stand on my own two feet and say yes to Jesus, the Holy Spirit, and the church.

Unfortunately, I just didn't get it. Maybe it was because the confirmation classes were not well taught, or the fact that I was just not ready and merely went through the motions to make sure "the Confirmation Box" was checked and my parents were pleased. Whatever the case, I missed it. I did not understand or appreciate who the Holy Spirit was, what the Holy Spirit did, or that the Holy Spirit was the ultimate power source and the key to supernatural living. Once I learned and discovered these things, everything changed!

The process of learning about the Holy Spirit began for me during my sophomore year in college, when I cried out to God for the first time in a personal and desperate way in the middle of lacrosse practice, right there on Cornell University's Schoellkopf Field.

It was in November of my junior year, nearly nine months after that spiritual birth or awakening, that my friend Jeff Caliguire shared a Bible verse that really challenged my thinking. It was from a letter the Apostle Paul wrote to the early church in Ephesus (modern-day Turkey) that says, "Do not get drunk on wine, which leads to debauchery. Instead, be filled with the Spirit."[5]

On Sunday nights, I would often go out to dinner with Jeff and ask him practical questions about living out this new spiritual life and relationship with God. After attending the fraternity/sorority Bible study that Jeff helped lead for a couple of months, it became clear to me that he and most of the attendees had a joy, excitement, depth, and power in their relationship with God that I lacked.

Although I was talking about my new faith with some of my teammates and friends, and actually inviting some of them to check out the Bible study, I knew I wasn't "all in" yet. And I wasn't having as much fun as I used to in the party and alcohol scene either. I felt like I was on a fence with one foot in the secular world, wanting to please my fleshly desires, and one foot in the spiritual world, wanting to please and enjoy the Lord. I was not experiencing the best of either. Sitting on a fence is never comfortable, and that was certainly true for me in this season of life.

During one of my Sunday night calls home, as I shared the tension in my heart and mind, my mom began to talk with me about the Holy Spirit.

"Frankie, you need to learn about the Holy Spirit," she advised.

A Blessing in Disguise

In early December, twenty of us from my fraternity, Chi Psi, planned to go to the George Thorogood concert on campus. He's the rock star best known for his hits *Bad to the Bone* and *I Drink Alone*. At the concert pre-party at Chi Psi, our fraternity brother who was handling the tickets realized he had only nineteen tickets, even though twenty of us planned to go. There was some real tension about who would be left out when I gave him my ticket back.

"I don't need to go," I said. "I have something else I can do."

The sold-out concert was on the same night as the Christmas party hosted by the fraternity/sorority Bible study and Cru. I made my way to the party, which turned out to be much better than I imagined and ultimately a blessing in disguise.

I ended up having a great conversation with a girl whose smile I can still see but whose name I can't remember. When I asked her if she knew anything about the Holy Spirit, she said, "Believe it or not, I just read a book about the Holy Spirit that was awesome, and I would be happy to give you a copy."

A few days later, she brought me a copy of *The Holy Spirit: The Key to Supernatural Living* by Bill Bright, the founder of Cru and Athletes In Action (AIA). As I read the book, light bulbs lit up in my mind. I was blown away by what I was learning and, multiple times, got up and walked around with tears in my eyes as I tried to comprehend this new paradigm, which, in time, would be life-changing.

I liked how the book noted there is no way, on this side of eternity, to fully comprehend the Trinity—Father, Son, and Holy Spirit—as one triune God. However, the analogy of H_2O being one chemical formula that can exist in three unique states, including water, ice, and steam, resonated with me.

I already felt like I had some understanding of God the Father and Jesus the Son. I had no trouble believing in Christmas or Easter, but I was ignorant and knew almost nothing about the Holy Spirit. Before, when I thought of the Holy Spirit, I thought of the classic movie *Star Wars* and the famous line, "May the Force be with you"—some nebulous cosmic force that moved about in the heavenlies. But I would soon learn a great deal more.

Who is the Holy Spirit?

Bright's book noted that although the Holy Spirit often seems to be the forgotten or neglected third person of the Trinity, the Bible has a lot to say about Him, including:[6]

- *The Holy Spirit is God and has the attributes of God.*
  I learned that the Holy Spirit is:
    o eternal and was present at the beginning of creation (Genesis 1:2)
    o omnipresent, or everywhere present (Psalm 139:7)
    o omniscient, or all-knowing (Hebrews 4:13)
    o omnipotent, or all-powerful (Matthew 19:26)

- *The Holy Spirit is a person, not just a force.*
  I learned that the Holy Spirit has traits that reflect His personality, including the reality that He can be:
    o obeyed (Acts 10:19-21)
    o lied to (Acts 5:3)
    o resisted (Acts 7:51)
    o grieved or saddened (Ephesians 4:30)
    o quenched (1 Thessalonians 5:19)
    o insulted (Hebrews 10:29)

- *The Holy Spirit is active all the time and does amazing things.*
  I learned that the Holy Spirit's actions reflect both the attributes of God and the characteristics of a person. For example, He:
    o speaks (Acts 13:2; Revelation 2:17)
    o teaches (John 14:26)
    o guides (John 16:13)
    o convicts—or makes us aware of our sin (John 16:7-8)
    o commands (Acts 8:29)
    o helps (Romans 8:26)
    o comforts (John 14:16, KJV)
    o performs miracles (Acts 8:39)
    o regenerates us (Titus 3:5)

o seals us in Christ (Ephesians 1:13)

o guarantees our inheritance (2 Corinthians 5:5)

o indwells us (1 Corinthians 6:19)

o fills us (Ephesians 5:18-20)

o produces fruit through us (Galatians 5:22-23)

In reading about the Holy Spirit, I also learned that He is referenced in the Scripture with what I like to call "nicknames," including *Comforter, Helper, Teacher, Guide, Counselor,* and *Advocate.* What an amazing resource we have been given access to if we choose to open our hearts, surrender our lives, and seek to be filled with the Holy Spirit.

Spiritual Poverty vs. Spiritual Power

I learned there are hindrances or obstacles that keep many people from experiencing the person and power of the Holy Spirit. These obstacles include:

- **Pride** (the mindset that we can live the Christian life in our own power)
- **Fear of man** (concern for what people will think if we get too into "this Jesus thing")
- **Worldly-mindedness** (believing in Jesus enough to make Him a part of our life, but not putting Him at the center of our life and instead focusing on all that the world has to offer)
- **Lack of faith** (not really believing or being willing to take the risk of believing in the Holy Spirit)
- **Ignorance or lack of knowledge** (simply not knowing the truth about the Holy Spirit)

The greatest obstacle or hindrance for me in not experiencing or plugging into the power of the Holy Spirit was a lack of knowledge. Like many others, and maybe you, I just didn't know who the Holy Spirit was, what the Holy Spirit did, or how to be filled with the Holy Spirit.

In his book, Bright shares a powerful story about a gentleman named Ira

Yates who owned a sheep ranch in West Texas during the Great Depression. As the story goes:

> Mr. Yates fell upon very difficult financial times, could not afford to pay the principal and interest on his mortgage, and was in real danger of losing his ranch. He had little money for clothes or food. His family, like many others during the Depression years, lived on government subsidies. Day after day, as Yates grazed his sheep over those rolling West Texas hills, he no doubt was greatly troubled about how he would be able to pay his bills. Then one day, a seismographic crew from an oil company came into the area and convinced Yates there might be oil on his land. They asked permission to drill a wildcat test well, and Yates signed a lease contract. At 1,115 feet underground, the drillers struck a huge oil reserve. The first well produced 80,000 barrels a day. Translated into today's market value, that's a gross income of about $2.5 million a day—from that single well—and that was only the beginning.
>
> The oil company dug many more wells, some more than twice as productive as the first. After oil had been pumped for more than 30 years, a government test of just one of the wells showed that it still had a potential flow of 125,000 barrels a day.
>
> The one-time sheep rancher named Yates owned it all. The day Yates purchased the ranch, he was very likely more interested in grazing land for his sheep than in the oil and mineral rights, which were also part of the purchase. There he was, living on government subsidy but sitting on a mammoth underground lake of incredibly valuable oil. He was a potential multimillionaire living in poverty. What was his problem? He simply did not know the oil was there.

Like Ira Yates with his sheep ranch, most people—including many Christians, like me many years ago—are unaware of the inexhaustible power and riches of God that are available to us through the Holy Spirit.

Many of us try to live the Christian life in our own power and experience frustration, guilt, fatigue, and little to no joy in our relationship with God. People are unaware of the incredible power source they can tap into, so they live in spiritual poverty.

When we tap into, connect with, and open our lives to the Holy Spirit, we can experience the abundant and fruitful life Jesus desires for us.

Bright reminds us that "Every day can be an exciting adventure for the Christian who has discovered the key to supernatural living. A person who surrenders their life to Jesus Christ and learns the reality of being filled with the Holy Spirit can live continually, moment by moment, under His gracious guidance and love. The Holy Spirit has come to give us a supernatural life that is more wonderful than the human mind can conceive or comprehend, and that supernatural life is available to you and me."

COMMAND AND PROMISE

Did you know that in the Bible, God *commands* us to be filled with the Holy Spirit, and He *promises* to fill us with the Holy Spirit if we surrender our lives to Him and, by faith, ask to be filled? Bright's book expounds on these two key words:

> The first word is *"command."* God commands us to be filled with the Holy Spirit. "Do not get drunk with wine, for this is dissipation. But be filled with the Spirit" (Ephesians 5:18). Therefore, to not be filled, controlled, and empowered by the Holy Spirit is disobedience.
>
> The second word is *"promise,"* which makes the command possible. "This is the confidence which we have before Him, that if we ask anything according to His will, He hears us. And if we know that He hears us in whatever we ask, we know that we have the requests which we have asked from Him" (1 John 5:14-15).
>
> Therefore, we can ask the question: "Is it God's will for you and me to be filled and controlled by the Spirit?" Yes, it is! God desires to see us filled with the Spirit because He loves us. It is His will, because it is His command.

The wonderful truth is that you and I can, right now, by faith, ask the Holy Spirit to fill us—not because we deserve to be filled, but on the basis of *God's command* and *His promise*.

Three Keys to Being Filled with the Holy Spirit

Most theologians would agree that if you have decided to believe, receive, and follow Jesus, the Holy Spirit already dwells within you. However, being fully surrendered to, filled with, baptized by, and plugged into the Holy Spirit is a different story.

I learned three keys to being filled with the Holy Spirit, which deeply challenged and helped me examine my own life, including:

1. The willingness to surrender every area of your life to the Lord.

Okay, I already gave Him the most important things to me at the time—football and lacrosse. I guess next would be the other areas of my life, like girls, the party scene, my future, etc. (Today, I regularly need to surrender my family, business, and other issues to the Lord.)

2. Confessing every known sin to the Lord and being willing to repent and choose God's best going forward.

I learned that once the Holy Spirit is in us, He promises never to leave us. Yet, I remember hearing an illustration that unconfessed sin is like a wet blanket on the flame of the Holy Spirit, quenching His power in and through us. I could relate to that.

Acknowledging my sin made me a little nervous because, *Hey, I am willing to confess my sin, but I don't think I can stop some of the things I'm doing like getting drunk with wine (or, in my case, other forms of alcohol), and other things I now know are not God's best, things that I now know are sin.*

My Bible study friends reminded me that I might not be able to change everything right away, but if I recognized and confessed my sin and told the Lord I was willing to change, the Holy Spirit would lead me and give me the power to choose God's best. I told the Lord that if He could change me and help me choose His best, I wanted that.

3. The willingness to give God your life and future and do whatever He leads or calls you to do.

I thought it would be okay to decide what I would do for the Lord and then ask Him to bless it. But God desires us to give Him our lives, and

He will lead us in what He created us to do. Was I willing to go all in and become anything God wanted me to be, or do? A priest? A missionary? Marry a woman I wasn't attracted to? (I had a distorted view of God's love and grace at that time.) I had surrendered lacrosse and my athletic career, but my whole life? God might mess it up.

As I continued to read and learn about the Holy Spirit and His power, I reached the point where I knelt on the rug next to my bed in our ugly house on Williams Street in College Town. Trembling with tears in my eyes, I prayed:

Lord, as You know, I surrendered my lacrosse and football career to You and invited You to come into my life and make me the person You want me to be back in February on Schoellkopf Field. Now tonight, I ask You to continue to cleanse me of my sin. I thank You for Your grace, mercy, and cleansing, and although I see areas of my life I don't think I can change, I am willing to change if You can change me. And this night, I want to fully surrender my life, my passions, my interests, and my future to You. If You want me to be a missionary to Africa or China or to become a priest—as much as that does not appeal to me right now—whatever You want, I want to do Your will. Now, Holy Spirit, please fill me. Amen!

After that prayer, I did not hear thunder or see lightning, but from that point forward, I began to see things happening around and through me that I now realize were the work of the Holy Spirit. This included having the courage to help start, lead, and invite friends and teammates to our new Bible study for athletes at my fraternity Chi Psi.

I still went to parties because I love people and having fun, and I still drank, but my twenty beers declined to fifteen, then ten, then six, until I was just nursing a couple. Once I experienced being filled with the Holy Spirit, God took away my desire to "get drunk with wine," and I learned I would much rather be filled with the Spirit than a cheap substitute.

Today, other things try to be "the wine" or "cheap substitute filler" of my life, but I try to keep a short account with the Lord (through confession) and daily ask for the fullness and power of the Spirit in my life.

Results of Being Filled with the Holy Spirit

Once I fully surrendered my life and future to the Lord and asked the Holy Spirit to fill me, I began to learn more and more about the results and impact of being filled. This is nothing you or I could ever take credit for, but amazing things happen if we choose to let the Holy Spirit fill us, lead us, and live through us.

How do we know if we are filled with the Holy Spirit?

We'll see evidence of the Spirit's work in our lives, which flows out of who He is and what He does.

The first results of the Spirit's filling for me were the illumination of the scriptures and a greater hunger for God's Word. I began to see and understand passages in the Bible that I'd never noticed or understood before.

My hunger and passion to read and study God's Word increased significantly. I remember walking across campus with a friend who graciously expressed concern that I was "taking this whole Bible thing too seriously." I thanked him for his concern and willingness to confront me as a friend, but explained that I now hungered for God's Word the way we hungered for pizza and wings on Friday nights after lacrosse practice.

"It is hard to explain," I said, "but I have found God's Word is like spiritual food for the Holy Spirit who now lives in me."

He probably thought I was crazy, yet to this day, we are good friends and still have faith-based conversations.

When we fully surrender our lives to the Lord and ask the Holy Spirit to fill us, He also promises to produce or bear His fruit through us—something called the Fruit of the Spirit. This includes the Lord's supernatural love, joy, peace, patience, kindness, goodness, faithfulness, gentleness, and self-control.[7] This fruit is so much greater than anything the world has to offer.

Another result of being filled with the Holy Spirit is having an increased desire and willingness to be a witness and share God's love and truth with others. The Holy Spirit empowers us to more fully love God, love others, and be a part of helping make disciples or new followers of Jesus.

Through the power of the Holy Spirit, I grew in my desire to obey and honor God and be a witness to the world in which I lived. I had never thought like that before. It had to be God's Spirit at work in and through me.

At first, being a witness meant trying to share God's love, truth, and what He had done in my life with those closest to me—like my family, friends, and teammates at Cornell.

Today, I desire to share God's love and truth, in both word and deed, with as many people as possible in Baltimore, the Mid-Atlantic region, across the country, and around the world. I need the fullness and power of the Holy Spirit to do that effectively.

When the Holy Spirit fills someone, He also gives them a spiritual gift or gifts to build up the Church or the body of Christ. These gifts can include wisdom, knowledge, faith, healing, teaching, prophecy, discernment, leadership, administration, exhortation, giving, evangelism, hospitality, helping, and shepherding.

No believer has all the spiritual gifts, but all followers of Jesus have a spiritual gift or gifts to bless and serve others. We are wise to keep our hearts and minds open to any spiritual gifts God has for us and not to put the Holy Spirit in a box.

Perhaps the most comforting result of being filled with the Spirit is an assurance about our relationship with God—a sense of confidence and peace about His presence in our lives.

In the Gospel of John, Jesus said, "The thief comes only to steal and kill and destroy; I came that they may have life and have it abundantly."[8] Through Jesus and the Holy Spirit who indwells us and lives through us, we can experience life to the full. God does not promise an easy life, but a full and abundant life with His peace that surpasses all understanding.

SPIRITUAL BREATHING

Toward the end of his book, Bright describes a practice called *spiritual breathing* that has helped me, and many others, be more continually filled with the Spirit.

Spiritual breathing, like physical breathing, is a process of exhaling the impure and inhaling the pure—an exercise in faith that enables you to continually experience God's love, grace, forgiveness, and power.

One of the things the Holy Spirit does is convict us, making us aware of sin in our lives. Spiritual breathing is a simple practice for followers of Jesus to acknowledge and confess sin as soon as we are aware of it and then reappropriate the fullness of the Holy Spirit in and through our lives.

When God makes you aware of a sin of commission (something you thought, said, or did that is not God's best or in alignment with His Word) or a sin of omission (something you didn't say or do when you should have), you acknowledge it, confess it, and ask for God's forgiveness.

Since God tells us in His Word that "if we confess our sins, He is faithful and just and will forgive us of our sins and purify us from all unrighteousness,"[9] you can acknowledge and receive His forgiveness and exhale your breath, as an expression of faith and a symbol of being cleansed from that sin. You then inhale your breath and ask God to refill you with the Holy Spirit, who lives in you and promises to never leave you.

It is then wise to thank God for His cleansing and forgiveness, and for refilling you with the Holy Spirit. Since God commands us to "be filled with the Spirit,"[10] we know it is His will for us to be filled. By faith, you can acknowledge and thank God for filling you with the Holy Spirit.

If you are breathing spiritually by exhaling (confessing your sin) and inhaling (appropriating the fullness of the Holy Spirit by faith), you can live and walk, minute by minute and hour by hour each day, in the fullness and power of the Holy Spirit.

What an exciting and supernatural way to live!

Five Prayers to Pray Every Day

Years ago, when people still listened to radio programs, I was working out in my basement and listening to a faith-based program with Dr. D. James Kennedy, a pastor of a large church in Florida. He shared five prayers that he prayed every day, which I found both simple and profound, and they aligned perfectly with spiritual breathing.

I have tried to pray them every day since:

1. Lord, please put to death my flesh and sinful nature.
2. Lord, please cleanse me of my sin(s). (Be as specific as you can.)
3. Lord, thank You for forgiving me and cleansing me of my sin(s).
4. Holy Spirit, please fill me and live through me.
5. Holy Spirit, thank You for filling me and living through me.

Through Dr. Kennedy's prayers, I also learned that we can pray to the Holy Spirit. I hadn't thought much about that before, but it makes sense because the Holy Spirit is God—the third person of the Trinity. We can pray to and call upon God the Father, Jesus the Son, and/or the Holy Spirit in any place and at any time.

PRAYER TO BE FILLED WITH THE HOLY SPIRIT

One way we express LOVE to others is by giving them gifts. One of the greatest gifts of love ever given or made available to us is the Holy Spirit and being filled with the Holy Spirit is the key to love and go with power, purpose, and fruitfulness.

Have you met God's conditions? Do you hunger and thirst for righteousness? Do you sincerely want to be filled, controlled, and empowered by the Holy Spirit? Are you willing to confess all known sins and surrender your life completely to the Lordship of Jesus Christ?

If so, bow your head and pray a prayer like the one on the next page, and watch the door to supernatural living open for you.

SUGGESTED PRAYER

Dear God,

I need You. I acknowledge that I've been in control of my life and that, as a result, I have sinned against You. I thank You, that You have forgiven my sins through Christ's death on the cross and the shedding of His blood for me. I now invite You to take control of my life and ask You to fill me with the Holy Spirit, as You commanded me to be filled, and as You promised in Your Word that You would do if I asked in faith. Holy Spirit, as an expression of my faith, I now thank You for filling me, taking control of my life, and empowering me to love and go as you live supernaturally through me.

In Jesus' name. Amen.

The Power of the Holy Spirit

TRUTH #4:
The key to supernatural living and fulfilling your
unique purpose in life is being plugged into God's power
by being filled with the Holy Spirit.

QUESTIONS FOR REFLECTION

1. How do you relate to the story about Ira Yates, the Texas cattle rancher living in poverty while not tapping into the abundant resource of oil on his property? Have you ever felt like you are living in "spiritual poverty," disconnected from the power of God? Explain.

2. What comes to mind when you read the verse in the book of Acts when Jesus said, "You will receive power when the Holy Spirit comes on you; and you will be my witnesses in Jerusalem, and in all Judea and Samaria, and to the ends of the earth?" Have you experienced that power?

3. Which nickname(s) for the Holy Spirit do you like best (*Comforter, Helper, Teacher, Guide, Counselor, Advocate*)? Why?

4. When you think of the fruit of the Holy Spirit, which do you most hope to see in your life (love, joy, peace, patience, kindness, goodness, gentleness, faithfulness, and/or self-control)?

5. Have you fully surrendered every aspect of your life to the Lord and asked the Holy Spirit to fill you? Why or why not?

6. What do you think about the discipline or practice of spiritual breathing?

The Power of Faith

TRUTH #5:

**Faith is a gift from God that can empower us
to overcome worry and fear and enable us to be and do
all that God created us to be and do.**

"So then faith comes by hearing, and hearing by the word of God."[1]

The Apostle Paul

After dating Gayle for about three years, when it became clear that our relationship was getting serious, she told me there was an important issue she wanted to discuss.

We decided to take a walk. At one point, she stopped, grabbed my hands, and her eyes teared up. She told me about a surgery she had during her senior year of high school that would likely limit her ability to get pregnant and have children. My heart pounded in my chest as I felt Gayle's pain, and my mind raced with thoughts of a future without children.

Courageously, she asked me to go with her to her doctor so I could fully understand all the issues and challenges we might face if we ever got married and wanted to have children together.

I loved Gayle, yet I knew I wanted to have children and a big family someday. I remember sharing the situation with my mom and dad. As usual, my mom gently shared perspective and grace, as my decision about possibly marrying Gayle would also affect them as potential grandparents.

"Frankie, do you love Gayle?" my mom asked.

"Yes, Mom, I do," I replied.

"Do you have faith and trust in God?" she asked.

Through tears, I said, "Yes, Mom, I think so."

My mom, understanding that her oldest son might knowingly marry a woman with a high chance of not being able to get pregnant, brought wisdom, faith, and love to the conversation.

I clearly remember the night I was driving to pick up Gayle to take her to dinner and then ask her to marry me. I had her parents' blessing, but in the back of my mind, I still had some doubts. I had prayed long and hard about this decision and knew I needed to rely on what little faith I had to overcome my fears.

After dinner at Sabatino's in Baltimore's Little Italy, on that cold, windy February night, we walked around the Inner Harbor and out onto a pier. There, I got down on one knee and asked Gayle to marry me. Fortunately, she said yes, and any fear I had disappeared. Since that moment, I have never doubted my decision to marry Gayle. I had to take that step of faith to receive God's blessing.

When we got married, we had no idea if or how we would have children, but I had peace. God, in His sovereignty, chose to bless us with two natural-born sons (with a little medical fertility assistance), as well as an adopted daughter and son. As of this writing, we also have two beautiful daughters-in-law and three grandsons.

It's amazing what God can do with even a little faith.

MUSTARD SEED FAITH

Jesus said, "...if you have faith as small as a mustard seed, you can say to this mountain, 'Move from here to there,' and it will move. Nothing will be impossible for you."[2]

Wow! What a bold statement—especially considering how small a mustard seed is, only about one to two millimeters (1/32 to 3/32 of an inch) in size. When I asked Gayle to marry me, I had a little faith; I guess I would call it "mustard seed faith."

I appreciate Rick Warren's reminder: "What matters is not the size of your faith but the size of the God you put it in. A little faith in a big God gets big results."[3]

And these words about faith (attributed to Dr. Martin Luther King Jr.) resonate deeply: "Take the first step in faith. You don't have to see the whole staircase to take the first step."

Sometimes that first step, no matter how small, is the hardest.

Faith, Trust, Belief

Webster defines faith as "belief and trust in, and loyalty to God." In the Bible, the words "faith," "trust," and "belief" are used interchangeably.

I can relate to times of having little faith, trust, or belief in God and His Word. I say I believe, but my thoughts and actions would indicate a lack of faith at times.

In the book of Hebrews, the writer—believed by some to be the Apostle Paul—says, ". . . without faith it is impossible to please God, because anyone who comes to Him must believe that He exists and that He rewards those who earnestly seek Him."[4]

I love the story in the Gospel of Mark about a father and his deeply troubled son. The father tracked down Jesus, and when the father finally found Him, he said:

> Teacher, I brought you my son who has a mute spirit. And whenever it seizes him, it throws him down, he foams at the mouth, gnashes his teeth, and becomes rigid. So, I spoke to your disciples that they should cast it out, but they could not.
>
> Jesus answered, "Bring him to me."
>
> Then, they took the son to Jesus. And when he [the boy] saw Him [Jesus], immediately the spirit convulsed him, and he fell to the ground and wallowed, foaming at the mouth.
>
> So, He [Jesus] asked the boy's father, "How long has this been happening to him?"
>
> The father responded, "from childhood. And often he has thrown himself into the fire and into the water to destroy him. But if you can do anything, have compassion on us and help us."
>
> "If you can?" said Jesus. "Everything is possible for one who believes."

Immediately, the father of the child cried out and said with tears,

"Lord, I believe; help my unbelief!"

Then Jesus rebuked the unclean spirit, saying to it, "'Deaf and dumb spirit come out of him and enter him no more.' Then the spirit cried out, convulsed him greatly and came out of him."[5]

Jesus set him free! Jesus healed the boy! Wow!

I love the humility of the father. He showed great faith by bringing his son to Jesus, yet in the same breath, in response to Jesus' statement about belief (faith), he said, "I believe," and "Help my unbelief."

That's me! I believe, yet I need help with my unbelief.

Can you relate?

A GIFT FROM GOD

In his letter to the early church in Ephesus, the Apostle Paul wrote, "For it is by grace you have been saved, through faith—and this is not from yourselves, it is the gift of God—not by works, so that no one can boast."[6]

By God's grace, or free and unmerited favor and blessing, the faith He allows us to have in Jesus is a gift. This gift is enough to cover our sins and save us from eternal separation from God. It also empowers us to welcome God and His presence into situations that only He can resolve.

Faith is truly a gift from God. Even when we lack belief or faith, God is faithful if we give Him the little mustard seed or remnant of faith that we do have.

I am reminded of the story of the French tightrope walker, Charles Blondin. In the summer of 1859, Blondin walked several times back and forth between Canada and the United States on a tightrope stretched over a quarter mile, spanning the breadth of Niagara Falls. He walked 160 feet above the thundering sound of the pounding water as huge crowds on both sides watched with shock and awe.

Blondin's feats were extraordinary. Once he crossed in a sack, another time on stilts, then on a bicycle. Once, he even carried a stove and cooked an omelet. On July 15 of that year, Blondin walked backward across the tightrope to Canada and returned to the United States pushing a wheelbarrow.

The story goes that after pushing the wheelbarrow across the tightrope while blindfolded, Blondin asked the crowd, "Do you believe I can carry a person across in the wheelbarrow?"

The crowd shouted, "Yes! We believe!"

Then he asked who would be willing to volunteer and get in the wheelbarrow. The crowd fell silent. No one stepped forward. Their belief or faith did not translate into total trust.

According to folklore, Blondin's manager, Harry Colcord, climbed onto Blondin's back as he pushed the wheelbarrow across the falls. Colcord had faith, trust, and belief in Blondin, and he showed it.

This story leads us to ask ourselves: Do I have the faith and belief to get into God's wheelbarrow and trust Him with my life?

Faith > Fear

How often have you and I had situations where we want to believe, we know we should believe, and all the evidence is there to believe and have faith, but instead, we are filled with worry or fear?

Fear and worry are the opposite of faith. Worry is focusing on our fears instead of trusting God. It is practical atheism, essentially, because we are thinking and acting as though we don't have a heavenly Father who has promised to care for our needs.

When we look back over our lives, we see that worry is worthless. It can't change the past or control the future; it can only make us miserable today. I have to remind myself that fear and worry don't change anything; only faith can do that.

I've heard it said, "Worry is like a rocking chair, it will give you something to do, but you don't get anywhere with it. Just think if every time we started to worry or fear, we would turn that worry or fear into a prayer. If we prayed about everything we worried about, we'd have a lot less to worry about."[7]

It's amazing to know there are more than 7,000 promises from God in the

Bible. When we pray in faith, believing for God's best, a great place to start is reading, believing, and claiming those promises. When we desire to turn our worries into prayer, we can use those promises to give words to our prayers.

One verse or promise in the Bible I quote to myself more than almost any other comes from a letter the Apostle Paul wrote to his dear friend and young mentee Timothy. Through Paul, the Holy Spirit reminds Timothy—and all of us—that, "God has not given us a spirit of fear, but of power and love and of a sound mind."[8] God's power and love are available to us at all times to calm our minds, give us peace, and help us overcome fear.

Many times, our fears don't make sense. What causes fear, anxiety, or worry for me might not bother you at all, and what causes fear, anxiety, or worry for you may be no big deal to me. The challenge for me, and probably you as well, is to place ourselves and our fears in God's wheelbarrow.

It's important to acknowledge that some people may have mental health conditions that make fear and anxiety uniquely challenging. Over the years, our daughter has experienced periods of clinical anxiety and depression, leading to some very difficult times and the need for wise counseling and medical assistance. But even if you're someone prone to such anxiety, depression, and fear, faith can help lead to greater peace, strength, and ultimately freedom.

Faith is greater than fear. As the Bible says, "There is no fear in love, but perfect love [God's love] casts out fear."[9]

It's interesting to note that "Fear not!" is the most repeated command in the Bible. In fact, it's been said that there are 365 "Fear nots" in the Bible—one "Fear not" for every day of the year!

Lloyd Ogilvie, in his book *Facing the Future without Fear*, notes there are actually 366 "Fear nots" in the Bible, one for every day of the year, including Leap Year. God doesn't want us to go a single day without hearing his word of comfort: "Fear not!"[10]

When our children were young, Gayle taught them a simple chorus they often sang before bed. It came from a Psalm that was penned by King David. It goes, "When I am afraid, I will trust in You, I will trust in You, I will trust in You. When I am afraid, I will trust in You, in God whose Word I praise."[11]

That's a great reminder and a Psalm worth singing.

LEAN NOT ON YOUR OWN UNDERSTANDING

I tend to be somewhat analytical and logical. Given the facts and necessary information, I can usually size up a situation pretty quickly and discern the best way forward.

However, there have been a number of situations over our family business' fifty-year history where things happened without warning and completely outside of our control that almost put us under. Each time, we were literally driven to our knees as a family to pray and seek God's wisdom, help, and protection. In those moments, we were reminded of the powerful words from Proverbs: "Trust in the Lord with all your heart, and lean not on your own understanding; in all your ways acknowledge Him, and He shall direct your paths."[12]

Trust in the Lord! Lean not on your own understanding! Acknowledge Him! And He will make your paths straight!

It was not about me, our family, or even our leadership team; it was about Him—the Lord. These verses are concise, clear and simple, but at times, they are very difficult to live out in business and other leadership roles.

The Bend in the Road vs. The End of the Road

In 1978, my dad, Francis X. Kelly Jr., decided to run for a State Senate seat in northern Baltimore County, Maryland. With five kids under the age of fourteen and a small business that he and my mother had started in our basement just two years prior, he decided to run, and he won. The legislative session met full-time from mid-January through mid-April each year in the state's capital, Annapolis.

He served three four-year terms, and during his third term, he was Vice Chairman of the powerful Budget and Taxation Committee. He was also rated as one of the top three most effective senators in the state.

In the fourth year of his third term—his twelfth year in office—a challenging political issue arose. A group of legislators introduced a bill that would allow abortion on demand through the ninth month of pregnancy, with no parental consent and no provision prohibiting school counselors from receiving financial incentives from pro-abortion organizations for referrals that led to abortions.

Whether you were pro-life or pro-choice, it was a bad bill. My dad led an eight-day filibuster, during which he and sixteen other state senators spoke around the clock, twenty-four hours a day, for eight straight days.

Before that legislative session in 1990, I had encouraged my dad—whom many of us call "Big Frank"—to read a Proverb each day of the session, as there are thirty-one proverbs in the book of Proverbs. He was on his second time through when Proverbs chapter 31, verse 8, jumped off the page and spoke to him: "Speak up for those who cannot speak for themselves..."

He knew he had to take a stand against this bad legislation, even if it cost him his senate seat. He and his colleagues' efforts killed the bill, but he did ultimately pay the price when, six months later, he lost in the primary election.

My dad knew in his heart that he had done the right thing. On the night of the primary election in September 1990, when the results came in at the campaign headquarters and showed he had lost, my dad stood and gave a gracious speech full of praise and thanksgiving to God—a true example of faith.

I then stood on a chair in the back of the room and shared how proud my family and I—and so many others—were of him. I said, "Dad, we know how much you loved your job in the State Senate, but I am reminded of the quote, 'We can see the bend in the road, and only God can see the end of the road.' You have trusted God, and it will be exciting to see how He blesses you and makes your path straight."

Ultimately, faith is more than just believing. Faith is more than thinking, talking, or even having convictions about Jesus. True faith leads to action. It is something you do, even if it comes at a steep price. My father modeled that for me and many others.

About three months after his election loss, we faced a significant, unforeseen business challenge, and my brothers and I would need Big Frank's time and presence to help us navigate it. Not having to deal with political commitments and responsibility in Annapolis freed him up to work with us.

An unfortunate error by our accounting firm from years past would require us to come up with money we didn't have, leading us to borrow from family, friends, and our retirement plans.

By God's grace, within two years, we paid back all our debts, with interest, and were better positioned for growth than ever before. Only God knew that we needed that challenging financial situation and time of pruning (we had to let ten of our thirty employees go) to help prepare us for rapid growth over the next twenty years: from about 1,000 corporate clients to more than 10,000, and from twenty employees to nearly 500.

A year after my dad's election loss, the first two of his grandchildren were born, including my son, Francis X. Kelly IV, who was a fertility miracle. Big Frank stood for life, and God blessed him with new life and many other blessings. Today, my mom and dad have twenty-one grandchildren and six great-grandchildren, with more on the way.

The Holy Spirit, through the prophet Jeremiah, wrote, "'For I know the plans I have for you,' declares the Lord, 'plans to prosper you and not to harm you, plans to give you hope and a future.'"[13]

And the Holy Spirit through the prophet Isaiah wrote, "'For my thoughts are not your thoughts, neither are your ways, my ways,' declares the Lord. '...As the heavens are higher than the earth, so are my ways higher than your ways and my thoughts than your thoughts.'"[14]

As we all know, things do not always work out the way we want, hope, or desire. But by faith, God's Word reminds us in different ways that while we can see to the bend in the road, only He can see to the end of the road.

FAITH COMES FROM HEARING

There is a famous quote attributed to St. Francis of Assisi that says, "Preach the gospel at all times, and if necessary, use words." That aligns with what James wrote in his letter by the same name, to the twelve tribes of Israel that "...faith without works is dead."[15]

Yet, the Holy Spirit, through the Apostle Paul's letter to the early church in Rome, reminds us that "...faith comes by hearing, and hearing by the word of God."[16]

When we share the Good News of God's love and truth, we must do so in both word and deed. While faith ultimately comes from hearing, believing, receiving, and applying God's Word to our lives, our faith must also be active and revealed by what we do and how we do it.

I've heard it said that if we believe, receive, and know God's Word well, we will have great faith. If we know God's Word, the Bible, a little, we will have a little faith, and if we neglect, reject, and don't know the Bible at all, we're not going to have any faith.

Faith is an expression of LOVE and only God can give us the kind of faith that overcomes worry and fear, enabling us to *love* and *go*, and be and do all that He created us to be and do.

SUGGESTED PRAYER

Dear God,

Thank You for the gift of faith. Please help me to believe, receive, and trust in You and Your Word. Please help me to love and go in faith and not fear. Please give me the faith and courage to share Your love and truth in both word and deed.

In Jesus' name. Amen.

The Power of Faith

TRUTH #5:

**Faith is a gift from God that can empower us
to overcome worry and fear and enable us to be and do
all that God created us to be and do.**

QUESTIONS FOR REFLECTION

1. Which quotes or stories in this chapter about faith resonated with you the most and why?

2. When you read the story from the Gospel of Mark about the father bringing his sick son to Jesus, what stands out to you about the father's faith? Can you relate to his statement, "I believe; help my unbelief"?

3. What in your life causes fear or anxiety? How do you try to apply faith to those situations or feelings?

4. What are your thoughts on the story of the famous French tightrope walker Charles Blondin and his wheelbarrow? Would you have gotten into his wheelbarrow and let him push you across a tightrope over Niagara Falls? More importantly, are you willing to get into "God's wheelbarrow" and trust Him with your life?

5. When you read and hear the scripture, "faith comes from hearing, and hearing from the word of God," what thoughts or feelings come to mind?

6. What do you think about Paul's words in his letter to the Ephesians: "For by grace you have been saved through faith—and this is not from yourself; it is the gift of God—not by works so that no one can boast"?

The Power of Wisdom

TRUTH #6:

True wisdom comes from God to help us live skillfully
and choose His best way forward.

"If any of you lacks wisdom, you should ask God, who gives generously to all without finding fault, and it will be given to you."[1]

James

The Bible is full of many amazing stories that are true based on historically validated evidence.

One of my favorite stories comes from a period approximately 1,000 years before the birth of Jesus Christ, when David, the second King of Israel, passed away and his young son Solomon was made king. One night, the Lord appeared to Solomon in a dream and said,

> "Ask for whatever you want Me to give you."
>
> Solomon answered, "You have shown great kindness to your servant, my father David, because he was faithful to you and righteous and upright in heart. You have continued this great kindness to him and given him a son to sit on his throne this very day.
>
> Now, Lord my God, you have made your servant king in place of my father David. But I am only a little child and do not know how to carry out my duties... So give your servant a discerning heart [wisdom] to govern your people and to distinguish between right and wrong. For who is able to govern this great people of yours?"
>
> The Lord was pleased that Solomon had asked for this. So God said to him, "Since you have asked for this [discernment/ wisdom] and not for long life and wealth for yourself, nor have asked for the death of your enemies but for discernment [wisdom]

in administering justice, I will do what you have asked. I will give you a wise and discerning heart, so that there will never have been anyone like you, nor will there ever be. Moreover, I will give you what you have not asked for—both wealth and honor . . ."[2]

God blessed Solomon with tremendous wisdom and wealth, and He even used Solomon to write the books of Proverbs and Ecclesiastes, both considered "wisdom" books in the Bible.

Since there are thirty-one Proverbs, a number of people I know read one Proverb each day of the month (e.g., Proverbs 3 on the third day of the month) to seek wisdom on a daily basis. Thousands of years after Solomon's life, the wisdom the Lord gave him still lives on and can bless us today if we choose to receive it, believe it, learn it, and live it.

DEFINING WISDOM

Webster's dictionary defines wisdom as "the soundness of an action or decision with regard to the appreciation of experience, knowledge, and good judgment."

Rick Warren defines wisdom as "seeing life from God's point of view or perspective, and making decisions the way God makes decisions."

My friend Mike Donohue Jr. defines wisdom as "living life skillfully."

I like all three definitions and think they complement each other. The good news is that God has promised to give us wisdom if we ask for it.

In the book of James, it says: "If any of you lacks wisdom, you should ask God, who gives generously to all without finding fault, and it will be given to you."[3]

Wisdom is really about perspective and how we see, understand, live, and ultimately communicate things. It's the filter through which we view and understand the world, and everyone's filter is a bit different.

To have true wisdom, godly wisdom, we need to see life through God's filter of truth. But how do we do that?

Many suggest that such wisdom and perspective come from our knowledge and understanding of God's Word, the Bible, and through revelation from the Holy Spirit.

Our wisdom worldview influences how we see everything—God, ourselves, others, the past, present, future, money, time, good, and evil. We all see and decide things based on our worldview filter, which we can hopefully learn to align with God's worldview.

Even when people are watching the same event, they often see it differently.

I appreciate the story about the first cosmonaut who entered outer space and circled the Earth. It was the 1960s, and he was part of the Soviet Union space program. At a press conference after he returned to earth, he said, "I searched the heavens and looked for God, and I did not see Him anywhere. Therefore, there is no God!"

About six months later, the United States sent an astronaut named John Glenn into space. He circled the earth three times, and after he returned, they held a press conference. Glenn said, "I saw God everywhere! I saw His glory in the galaxy. I saw His splendor in the universe. I saw His majesty in the stars."

Both men were brilliant, courageous, and well-trained. One had godly wisdom and perspective in seeing truth; the other did not.

First Word/Last Word

Although the media can provide important information and perspective, we must remember that we don't get wisdom from newspapers, magazines, the internet, or television. True wisdom comes from God and His Word.

Rick Warren reminds us, "If you want to become wise, the first thing you have to do is feed yourself God's Word every day."[4]

Each morning, I have three different devotionals automatically emailed to me—*Daily Hope* by Rick Warren, *Daily Practice* from ChurchNativity.com, and *Jesus Calling* by Sarah Young. Each one includes a scripture or verse from the Bible and a reflection or perspective on that scripture. Before I even get out of bed or check my email or text messages, I try to read, receive, and reflect on God's Word. It's spiritual food that feeds the Holy Spirit in me.

Each evening as I lie in bed, the last thing I try to read and reflect on is a Bible verse or two from the Bible app. This again feeds the Spirit in me and helps me rest, as God's Word permeates and settles my heart and mind with truth and wisdom. Scripture tells us, ". . . for He grants sleep to those He loves."[5]

My goal is for God to have the first and last word of each day that He blesses me with.

More than just a quick word in the morning or at night, I have also found it to be extremely valuable to read, study, and meditate on God's Word on a regular basis. There are many amazing Bible study guides, programs, and in-person and online classes like Bible Study Fellowship (BSF) and Community Bible Study (CBS). I love CBS's mission "to make disciples of the Lord Jesus Christ . . . through caring, in-depth Bible study for all."

Whatever the Bible study program or guide, the key is to remember that the Bible is full of truth and wisdom to help us live life skillfully and make good decisions in a world full of rip currents that want to push and pull us in all kinds of dangerous directions.

I've heard it said, "The only way to be wise is to walk with God. And to walk with God, you need to spend time reading and studying His Word—the Bible. There are no shortcuts to wisdom."[6]

My friends Dan Britton and Jimmy Page, in their book *Wisdom Walks*, talk about something they call GIGO—Garbage In, Garbage Out.[7] There are countless opportunities every day to feed our hearts and minds with poison or junk food that will negatively impact different areas of our lives.

Truth is health food for our minds, so wise people feed on truth. Wise people also invite other wise people into their lives, which today can not only be done by having wise friends but through good books and good podcasts as well. It is so true, "While it is wise to learn from experience, it is wiser to learn from the experience of others."[8]

God's Word reminds us, "Whoever walks with the wise becomes wise, but the companion of fools will suffer harm."[9]

Opposites and Paradoxes

There are many in our society who hold academic degrees, are highly educated, and even have positions of influence, but they are not wise.

The opposite of wise people are fools. In the book of Proverbs, we read, "The fear of the Lord is the beginning of knowledge [and wisdom], but fools despise wisdom and instruction."[10]

I know I don't want to be a fool, yet God's ways of wisdom often seem so different from the world's and from most of my natural inclinations.

I want to be first, not last, but God's Word says, "...the last will be first, and the first will be last."[11]

I want to be strong, not weak, but God says in His Word, "My grace is sufficient for you, for my power is made perfect in weakness." Then the Apostle Paul writes, "For when I am weak, then I am strong."[12]

I want to take charge and be in control of my own destiny to the extent that I can, yet God's Word reminds us "to offer your bodies as a living sacrifice, holy and pleasing to God..."[13]

At many high school and college graduations, you hear speakers proclaim, "You can be, do, and accomplish anything you want with your life," which sounds good, but we all know it is not true.

No matter how hard I tried, I could never have been a professional basketball player and star in the NBA. I think a better, wiser message is: "You can be and do anything God created you to be and to do."

God says, in His Word, if we ask Him for wisdom, which is His best way forward, He will give it to us.

Surrender to Win

A number of years ago, several of us helped my dad write a book about his life called *Surrender to Win*. Talk about opposites. In the book, my dad shares his story of family and faith and how, by God's grace, he overcame his battle with alcoholism. His dad (my grandfather) and his grandfather (my great-grandfather) also battled alcoholism, or what some call the "Irish Virus."

Through the twelve steps of Alcoholics Anonymous (AA), my dad got sober. About two years after his last drink, he ultimately surrendered his life to the Lord and found freedom not only from his addiction but also from the anxiety and fear that led him to drink.

Every day, we have to decide who's going to be in control of our lives—us or God. Rick Warren writes, "The number one reason we're under stress is we're trying to control things that only God can control.[14] When we think about life, we really can't control much of anything, including our spouse, kids, job, future, or even our past. When God is at the center of your life, you worship; when He is not, you worry."[15]

That is true wisdom!

I believe one of the greatest "wisdom prayers" of all time is known as the AA Prayer, or the Serenity Prayer, which begins:

God, grant me the serenity
to accept the things I cannot change,
courage to change the things I can,
and wisdom to know the difference.[16]

Freedom, joy, and power come when we surrender whatever we have been trying to control back to God. Then, we will know and experience God's wisdom, peace, and joy. In a world that teaches us to fight and battle for what we want, God's Word challenges us to surrender our lives and issues to Him in order to win.

We are also called to thank God for our weaknesses because, when we are weak, He can be strong through us. And, we are challenged to put others before ourselves because, when we are last, in God's eyes, we are ultimately first. Wisdom is ultimately about love, and wisdom shows up in relationships.

I have to continually remind myself that God's Word says, "For my thoughts are not your thoughts, neither are your ways my ways," declares the Lord. "As the heavens are higher than the earth, so are my ways higher than your ways and my thoughts than your thoughts."[17]

WISDOM WARNINGS

God's Word has so much to say about living life skillfully, including what I call "Wisdom Warnings." Most of those warnings begin with the words "Do not," but all are written and shared to ultimately bless and protect us. There are many Wisdom Warnings in the Bible, but several really stand out to me, including:

Do Not Judge: "Do not judge, or you too will be judged. For in the same way you judge others, you will be judged, and with the measure you use, it will be measured to you."[18]

Judging is what I have come to learn is a "boomerang sin." Whenever we judge another person without knowing all the facts, that judgment often comes back on the person who made the judgment. And getting hit in the face with a boomerang can be very painful, to say the least.

Rick Warren says, "Wise people don't emphasize others' mistakes; instead, wise people are merciful. Wise people cut people slack because they know God cuts them slack all the time."[19]

When we judge, we are being foolish. When we are merciful, we are being wise and reflecting God. Judging is God's job, not ours. For us, judging is a sin that keeps on giving. We are wise to extend grace and mercy and not to judge others.

Do Not Repay Evil for Evil: "Do not repay anyone evil for evil. Be careful to do what is right in the eyes of everyone . . . Do not be overcome by evil, but overcome evil with good."[20]

Our human nature wants to repay evil with evil. Evil is often referred to as darkness, and as Dr. Martin Luther King Jr. said, "Darkness cannot drive out darkness; only light can do that. Hate cannot drive out hate; only love can do that."[21]

Wisdom brings light into areas of darkness. Jesus said, "I am the light of the world. Whoever follows me will never walk in darkness, but will have the light of life."[22] When we walk in wisdom, we bring Jesus—and thus light—into challenging, evil, and dark situations.

Do Not Get Drunk: "Do not get drunk on wine, which leads to debauchery. Instead, be filled with the Spirit."[23]

This verse really spoke to me in college. In my freshman and sophomore years, I passionately challenged the first half of this scripture. In my junior and senior years, I learned and began to live out the second part of it. Based on experience, I can tell you that I would much rather be filled with the Holy Spirit than alcohol or any other cheap substitute.

It is interesting to note that the first public miracle Jesus performed was turning water into wine at a family wedding. Clearly, Jesus didn't hate wine; He just didn't want us getting drunk on wine or alcohol because that quenches His best for us, which is being filled with the Holy Spirit.

We can discern and embrace God's wisdom when we are filled with the Holy Spirit.

Do Not Let Unwholesome Talk Come Out of Your Mouths: "Do not let any unwholesome talk come out of your mouths, but only what is helpful for building others up according to their needs."[24] We must remember that "our tongues have . . . the power of life and death."[25]

Although our tongue is a small part of our body, it can be like a small spark that sets an entire forest on fire. Can you relate? I can!

The tongue really refers to our words, and we are wise to *T.H.I.N.K.* before we speak. Ask, are my words or what I am about to say, *Thoughtful, Honest, Important, Necessary,* and *Kind?* We are wise to pause, pray, and think before we speak.

Be Slow to Anger: "Everyone should be quick to listen, slow to speak and slow to become angry."[26]

My natural inclination is to be quick to speak, slow to listen, and relatively quick to judge or get angry. One mark of a wise person is someone who asks good questions and then listens. God gave us two ears and one mouth. We always learn more when we are listening than when we are talking.

We are wise to remember, "The Lord is compassionate and gracious, slow to anger, abounding in love."[27]

WISDOM CALLINGS

God's Word doesn't just tell us what *not* to do. He is not a cosmic killjoy who wants us to be miserable or bored. In His wisdom, God also calls us to exciting opportunities because, at the end of the day, He loves us, He is for us, and He wants what is best for us. It's up to us to respond to what I call His "Wisdom Callings."

Come To Me: "Come to Me, all of you who are weary and burdened, and I will give you rest."[28]

What an awesome invitation! The Creator of the universe literally calls us by name to come to and have a relationship with Him. We are being wise when we turn to Jesus and bring Him our anxieties, burdens, and fears.

My tendency is not to want to bother God with "my stuff," but ultimately, He knows and cares about everything happening in our lives. He always welcomes and invites us to come to Him with any and every concern. If we choose to come to Him, we can experience His rest and peace, which is far greater than anything the world can offer or provide.

Follow Me: "Follow Me, and I will make you fishers of people."[29]

Jesus calls us to follow Him, and if we do, we will become part of His master plan to help others become disciples, or followers, of Him as well.

We are wise to follow this call and help those in our sphere of influence come to know and experience God's love, grace, truth, and plan for their lives.

If we choose to heed the call to become Jesus' followers, we can be a part of God's eternal plan of redemption and hope for all people—a wise decision with significant eternal impact.

Trust Me: "Trust in the Lord with all your heart and do not lean on your own understanding. In all your ways acknowledge Him, and He will make your paths straight."[30]

These verses of Scripture are often easier said than done, but we are exercising wisdom when we choose to "trust in the Lord..., lean not on our own understanding..., and acknowledge God in all our ways..." When we decide to trust and acknowledge God, He promises that "He will make our paths straight."

I don't know how it works, but I pray God gives me the faith and wisdom to trust and acknowledge Him and see Him work in powerful ways. This is definitely a different kind of wisdom and thinking than the world offers.

Delight in Me: "Delight yourself in the Lord; and He will give you the desires of your heart."[31]

To "delight yourself in the Lord" means to seek and find peace, hope, fulfillment, and satisfaction in Him. It is so easy to delight in success, wealth, status, and material possessions, but when we are wise, we delight in the Lord.

If we choose to delight ourselves in the Lord, He promises to give us the desires of our hearts. This certainly does not mean God will give us everything we want. I believe it means that, if we choose wisely to delight in the Lord, He will align our hearts and passions with His.

God knows the depths of our hearts and desires much more intimately than we do. When we truly delight in Him, we will walk and live in true peace, joy, and fulfillment.

Come to Me, Follow Me, Trust Me, Delight in Me—these are wise callings I desire to respond to. How about you?

CONFIRMED IN THREES

I have a good friend and business associate who is an amazing magician. He is a strong follower of Jesus, so his magic is not connected to the occult in any way, but he is uniquely gifted in what is known as "sleight of hand."

His card tricks are amazing, and his ability to play the "shell game" is unparalleled.

The shell game involves three shells and a small red ball. He places the ball under one shell and asks you to watch closely. Then, he slides and shifts the shells around quickly before asking which shell the ball is under.

If you watch closely, it should be easy to guess where the ball is, but it's not. He can even make the ball disappear completely, not appearing under any of the shells. Or, he can make multiple balls appear under one or all of the shells.

Can you relate to sometimes feeling like finding God's wisdom or will for an important decision is like playing the shell game? Do you ever wonder if God is purposely keeping you from His wisdom or the best way forward?

Regardless of how we feel, it is a blessing to know that if we lack wisdom, we can ask God, and He authentically wants to guide us and give us the wisdom we need to make the best decision.

For some reason, there are times when God's wisdom and best way forward seem very slow in coming and not completely clear. Some situations and decisions require such wisdom that God wants and needs us to slow down. Some decisions Gayle and I have had to make have even required prayer and fasting, taking a break from food and pleasures to better focus and hear God's still, quiet voice.

For serious decisions that require great discernment and wisdom, prior experience, and, more importantly, God's Word has taught me that He often confirms His will and best way forward in threes. Some decisions are not just holy; they are holy, holy, holy.

From the Trinity (three persons, one God) to Jesus rising on the third day, the number three in the Bible often conveys themes of divine protection, completeness, and God's profound involvement in the world or even a specific situation.

In 2004, Gayle and I received an email from Catholic Charities Adoption Services about a need for a family to adopt a young boy. I guess our name ended up on their list after we adopted our daughter Jackie from South Korea several years earlier.

When Gayle called to inquire about the situation, they realized they had emailed us by mistake. However, since Gayle replied, they said, "We are not supposed to contact you about an adoption need unless you inquire, but since you have called us, would you be open to considering a specific adoption need in the future?"

Gayle told them, "Let me talk to my husband and get back to you." After some casual prayer and discussion, we decided to call them back and let them know we were very happy with our current family of three children. However, we said that if a significant need arose and no one else stepped up, we would at least be willing to pray about it.

A month later, the call came. There was a two-year-old boy in South Korea who had lived with his birth mother for a year and a half and had spent the last six months between an orphanage and a foster family. Would we be willing to adopt him?

Oh boy! Gayle and I discussed it and decided we would at least pray about it. We also decided to involve our three children in the decision, as it would significantly impact all of us.

One day, we held a family meeting in the treehouse in our backyard. We had never all been up there together before (or since, by the way), but I thought it would be a relaxed place to have such a serious discussion.

Frankie was fourteen, Stephen was eleven, and Jackie Lee was eight at the time. Gayle and I were both open to the idea, especially since we were so thankful for our adoption of Jackie Lee when she was six months old.

We were in a great place as a family—out of the diaper and car seat stage—but I had often made half-joking, half-serious comments during family dinners about the empty chair. For years, we ate around our rectangular wooden country table, which had two seats on each long side and one seat at each head. I always sat at one head and Gayle at the other, while the kids sat with two on one side and one on the other. Very often, after saying grace or while eating, I would see the one empty seat and say, "I feel like someone is missing." I had been saying this for years when we mistakenly received that email from Catholic Charities Adoption Services.

Perched in the treehouse, I started with our oldest. "Frankie, what do you think?"

He quietly replied, "Do what you think is best, but I really like our family the way it is."

"Thanks, Frankie," we replied.

Then I turned to Stephen, who, at the time, was probably the most self-focused of our crew. To Gayle's and my surprise, Stephen said, "He can have my bed! I will sleep on the floor. I definitely think we should adopt him."

Wow! What a bold response.

Finally, we turned to Jackie Lee. As our youngest, she was kind of shy, and by nature, an introvert. With little tears in her beautiful black Korean eyes, she said, "I like our family the way it is too. But who am I to say no to adopting this boy when you didn't say no to me?"

Wow! By then, we were all in tears.

That night, I decided I would pray and fast (not eat any food) over the weekend since we had to give Catholic Charities our answer by Monday morning. Gayle and I were not sure, as this decision would significantly impact each of us, our family dynamic, and our future.

Although fasting was not a discipline I practiced often, when I did, I experienced real clarity. I prayed and asked God to please give us wisdom and confirm our decision beyond a shadow of a doubt.

I fasted all day on Friday. Later that evening, I took Frankie, Stephen, and Jackie to our community pool. Very few people were there when a woman came up to me out of nowhere and started asking about our kids, who were all swimming together in the shallow end. She noticed Jackie and asked if she was adopted.

I said, "Yes, we adopted her from South Korea."

She then shared that she had two adopted children—a girl first, then a boy—and said, "It has been fantastic!"

That was interesting, I thought, but I didn't even mention it to Gayle that night when we got back to the house. The next day, we ended up back at the pool in the late afternoon.

Again, it was not crowded, and I was talking to the lifeguard, who was a family friend, when another woman I didn't know approached me. She asked about Jackie and got excited when I told her she was adopted from South Korea. She shared that her friend had adopted two children from Korea—a girl first, then a boy—and said, "It's the best decision they ever made."

This time, when I went home, I had to share it with Gayle. Was God confirming this?

On Sunday, our family was invited to a cookout at another pool. (I hadn't been to a pool three days in a row since I was a young boy.) Even though I wasn't eating, I was walking around the pool area when I saw a friend in the water holding her newborn baby. I congratulated her, and she yelled back, "Hey Frank, we now have four children, just like you!"

I replied, "We don't have four, we only have three!"

She then said, "I thought for sure you had four children. All I know is when I see you and Gayle, I see four children."

I couldn't believe it. Three confirmations in three days. Immediately, I made my way over to Gayle, shared what happened, and said, "Call Catholic Charities in the morning. Let's adopt this boy."

The day after Christmas 2005, our family boarded a plane from Dulles International Airport in Washington, D.C., to Incheon International Airport in Seoul, South Korea. I'll never forget the day we met our new son at the Holt International Adoption Agency. His name was Kim Joo Yung. He had experienced a lot of transitions in his young life.

We decided to rename him Joseph Kim Kelly. Kim was his Korean surname, Joseph was close to Joo, and we loved the Josephs we had read about in the Bible. It didn't take long before we all started calling him JK.

The first couple of weeks after we returned home were very difficult. JK was distraught and despondent. At two and a half years old, he spoke no English, loved Korean food, and had never seen so many white people in his life. We began to doubt our decision, but we knew God had confirmed it supernaturally three times.

As of this writing, JK is a senior at Cornell University. As a junior, he was fortunate to be a defenseman on the men's Big Red Lacrosse team that won the 2025 NCAA Division I National Championship. He is a hardworking, thoughtful, and kind young man. We cannot imagine our family without him.

God's ways, will, and wisdom are so much greater than ours, and He loves to reveal them to us if we ask. No shell game!

THE WAYS OF WISDOM

Godly wisdom gives us discernment, direction, and perspective, and reminds us that:

- When we are wise, we see things the way God sees things.

- When we are wise, we follow God's way forward.

- When we are wise, we don't judge, and our words are measured to help build others up.

- When we are wise, we listen more than we speak, and we don't get easily offended.

- When we are wise, we offer others grace and mercy, and we don't return evil for evil but instead help shine light in the darkness.

- When we are wise, we live with an eternal mindset and perspective.

I love the quote from the Roman general Maximus, in the Academy Award-winning historical fiction movie *Gladiator*, when he says, "What we do in life echoes in eternity."

At the end of the day, wisdom reminds us that life is not just about you or me. It's about God, our Creator, and His love, truth, and purpose. Ultimately, we need God's wisdom to *love* and *go* with an eternal mindset while living life skillfully and choosing His best.

DO IT ANYWAY

One of the wisest women to have ever lived was Mother Teresa of Calcutta, who founded the Missionaries of Charity. This incredible organization grew to include more than 4,500 nuns serving the "poorest of the poor" in more than 130 countries.

There is so much that could be written or said about her life and legacy, but if there was one word to describe her, it would be LOVE.

I thought a great way to close this chapter on God's wisdom and ways was to share a poem widely attributed to her, "Do It Anyway."

People are often unreasonable, irrational, and self-centered.
Forgive them anyway.

If you are kind, people may accuse you of selfish, ulterior motives.
Be kind anyway.

If you are successful, you will win some unfaithful friends
and some genuine enemies.
Succeed anyway.

If you are honest and sincere, people may deceive you.
Be honest and sincere anyway.

What you spend years creating, others could destroy overnight.
Create anyway.

If you find serenity and happiness, some may be jealous.
Be happy anyway.

The good you do today will often be forgotten tomorrow.
Do good anyway.

Give the best you have, and it will never be enough.
Give your best anyway.

In the final analysis it is between you and God;
it was never between you and them anyway.

SUGGESTED PRAYER

Dear God,

Thank You for Your promise that if I seek wisdom from You, You will give it to me. Please give me Your wisdom and help me love and go skillfully, seeing things from Your perspective and choosing Your best ways forward.

In Jesus' name. Amen.

The Power of Wisdom

TRUTH #6:

**True wisdom comes from God to help us live skillfully
and choose His best way forward.**

QUESTIONS FOR REFLECTION

1. After reading this chapter, how would you define wisdom? Do you truly believe that "if you lack wisdom, you can ask God who gives generously . . . and it will be given to you?"

2. If you could ask for anything and it would be given to you, what would you ask for? What did Solomon ask for, and how did that work out for him?

3. What struck you about the story of the cosmonaut from the Soviet Union and the astronaut (John Glenn) from the United States?

4. Which "Wisdom Warning" spoke most to you? Why?

5. Which "Wisdom Calling" spoke most to you? Why?

6. Share an experience or time where you believe God gave you His supernatural wisdom. What is something you need God's wisdom for at this time?

PART TWO

GO

The Power of Purpose

TRUTH #7:

**God has a unique purpose for you
and living for His purpose will abundantly bless your life
on earth and your eternal destiny forever.**

*"And we know that in all things God works for the good of those who love
Him, who have been called according to His purpose"*[1]

The Apostle Paul

Purpose is defined as the reason for which something is done, created, or for which something exists. A root question behind purpose is: Why?

Have you ever wondered why you were created or born? I believe only God knows the full answer to that question, but He gives us plenty to consider and embrace from His Word.

After I graduated from Cornell, I went on a summer mission trip to Japan with Athletes in Action (AIA) and Cru. We spent time in Tokyo and Okinawa, teaching college students English, building relationships, and playing basketball, and even some lacrosse with them. During that trip, I interviewed about the possibility of a full-time international staff position with AIA.

Through my Cornell Bible study experience and summer mission in Japan, I have come to learn and believe that only three things last forever. Those three eternal things are God, His Word, and the souls of men and women. To the extent that I would invest my life in these three things, I would be investing in eternity and could have an eternal purpose and impact.

For years, my purpose had been athletic prowess and academic achievement. My thinking was that I would graduate from Cornell, pursue a joint MBA/law degree, and climb the ladder of worldly success and adulation. I believed I could transfer my competitive sports and scholastic mindset to the corporate or political world and prove my worth and value. These aspirations weren't bad in themselves, but as I began to study and learn more, my paradigm or worldview was being tested.

As I reflected more and more on Jesus' words, I was challenged in my heart and mind to better understand what it really meant to build treasure in heaven that would last forever.

Jesus said, "Do not store up for yourselves treasures on earth, where moth and rust destroy, and where thieves break in and steal. But store up for yourselves treasures in heaven, where neither moth nor rust destroys, and where thieves do not break in or steal..."[2]

Reading about missionaries like C.T. Studd and his six Cambridge University classmates (known as the Cambridge Seven), who gave up great family wealth and prestige as highly regarded student-athletes to go and share God's love and truth in Africa and India, and Jim Elliott, a star wrestler in college who died trying to share the Good News with the Huaorani people, or Auca tribe of Ecuador, inspired me to consider an eternal mindset instead over a temporal one.

C.T. Studd wrote, "Only one life, 'twill soon be past, only what's done for Christ will last."[3] And Jim Elliott famously said, "He is no fool who gives what he cannot keep, to gain what he cannot lose."[4]

What would happen if I chose to live and invest my life—my time, talent, and treasure—with a more eternal perspective and purpose than a temporal one?

AN ETERNAL PERSPECTIVE AND INTEGRATED LIFE

When I flash back to my post-graduation summer mission trip to Japan, I will never forget that Sunday after church when a group of us went to a beach in Okinawa for some sun, fun, and a little rest.

I had brought my Bible in my backpack and, later in the day, decided to take some quiet time for reflection. By chance (or what I like to call "God-incidence"), I turned to the book of Acts, which is the first book in the Bible after the four Gospels, and started to read the first chapter.

In verse 8, I came across the last words Jesus spoke to His followers. It was forty days after His resurrection, and right before He ascended into heaven, when He said, "...You will receive power when the Holy Spirit has come upon you; and you shall be My witnesses both in Jerusalem, and in all Judea and Samaria, and even to the remotest part of Earth."[5]

For some reason, the words of this one verse jumped off the page. I had learned about and experienced the power of the Holy Spirit during my junior year at Cornell, and God had given me a great passion to be a witness to His love, grace, and truth. But for some reason, the word that first hit me that day was *Jerusalem*.

There I was in Japan, which, for a kid from Baltimore who had rarely traveled out of the country, seemed like one of the "remotest parts of Earth," yet God gave me a strong sense that He wanted me to go back home and start my ministry or work in my Jerusalem—Baltimore.

Still sitting on the beach, another word came to me. It wasn't audible, but it was clear: *Business*.

Hmm. What does that mean? I thought to myself.

During my senior year, I had interviewed with great companies like Procter & Gamble and MBNA (now Bank of America), but I didn't feel any interest or passion for the corporate world.

Before graduation and leaving for Japan, my dad asked me to consider coming home to Baltimore to work in the small insurance business he and my mom had started in the basement of our family home ten years earlier. He felt God had blessed them with the business, and he said he would love for his oldest son to spend at least one year in the business before going off to save the world.

When he suggested that before my trip to Japan, I thought, *No way!*

But that day on the beach, I got a very strong impression that I was supposed to honor my dad's request. I thought to myself, *I guess I could waste one year of my life working with my mom and dad in something as eternally insignificant as a small insurance and benefits company.* (Although I would soon learn there is no eternally insignificant work if it's done in an effort to honor and serve God and others.)

After having clear impressions about the words *Jerusalem* and *Business,* the words *School, Lacrosse,* and *Friends* came to me in successive order. I didn't know what they meant at the time, but over the years, I would find out.

When I returned to Baltimore, I thanked my dad for supporting me on the summer mission trip and told him I felt called to honor his request and work in the business for a year. He was thrilled to have his oldest son working as a salesperson.

"Frank, this is great," he said. "As I told you before, our business is all about relationships, and you can impact many lives. You will have a tough job to do, but you won't have to punch a clock, so you can have great flexibility with your time. Flexibility gives you quality of life, which is more important than money. You can be in business, still be an ambassador for the Lord's love and truth, and have the flexibility to do things outside the business as well."

That fall, I also went back to my high school, Calvert Hall, and convinced the administration to let me start a Bible study or fellowship for athletes, as a new club option. They reluctantly agreed, and we started after the first of the year. Before I knew it, a couple of dozen guys (Calvert Hall is an all-boys school) were showing up for what we first called AIA, but later changed to an FCA Huddle. The names or initials didn't really matter, but FCA's mission "to lead every coach and athlete into a growing relationship with Jesus Christ and His church" was a better fit for what we were trying to accomplish. I would learn that mission (or purpose) statements matter.

One morning after our Calvert Hall FCA Huddle meeting, I was walking through the hallway when my former high school lacrosse coach, Mike Thomas, asked if I could be his main assistant on the varsity lacrosse team that spring. Later that day, I asked my dad, who was now my boss as well, if I could take the role. He reminded me of the value of a family business and told me I had the flexibility to do it as long as I got my job done. I would have to leave the office by 3 p.m. each day, but could make up the time early in the morning or at night.

Soon after I started coaching each weekday afternoon, a new professional indoor lacrosse league launched, and I was picked up by the Baltimore Thunder. Before I knew it, I was coaching high-level high school lacrosse, playing professional indoor lacrosse, and helping start lacrosse at an FCA sports camp in Gettysburg, Pennsylvania, as well as an FCA Lacrosse Coaches Breakfast at the annual US Lacrosse Coaches Convention. I guess my lacrosse career wasn't over after college.

Doors also opened for me to start several small group Bible studies for a number of my former middle school and high school friends, as well as other associates who were open to learning.

About six months after I started working in our family business, known then as Kelly-Chick & Associates, I found myself just going through the motions of business. That's when I was challenged by a scripture that says, "Whatever you do, work at it with all your heart, as working for the Lord, not for human masters, since you know that you will receive an inheritance from the Lord as a reward."[6]

I had only six months left to honor my commitment to my dad to work at least one year in the family business, and I was convicted that it was time to give my best effort. At the end of the day, I wasn't working for my mom and dad or the business; I needed to be giving my best effort as if working for the Lord.

I learned that God doesn't necessarily care *what* we do (as long as it is a job that doesn't violate His Word), but *how* we do it. I could be a janitor, a teacher, a lawyer, a doctor, a truck driver, or a businessperson and still be fulfilling God's purpose for my life.

I was learning there was no difference between what some might call "sacred" work and "secular" work. Working full-time in a church or faith-based ministry is not more important than working in a secular job, as long as my motive and goal to honor and glorify God are the same. I realized I could be in the marketplace, or be a teacher and coach, and be just as committed to sharing God's love and truth as a priest, pastor, or full-time missionary.

I recall being encouraged to keep my priorities in good order—make my relationship with God first, my wife second, my children third, and my work and hobbies fourth and fifth on my priority list. That was wise counsel, but another, more integrated way I learned to view and live out those priorities was to keep God or Jesus at the center of every area in my life. Jesus at the center of my relationship with God the Father; Jesus at the center of my relationship with Gayle; Jesus at the center of my relationship with our children; Jesus at the center of my work or vocation; Jesus at the center of my coaching, playing lacrosse, hobbies, or whatever was important in my life.

The challenge was to live an integrated life, where Jesus was at the center of everything I did—not just once a week at church or during Bible study. I learned that God doesn't view what we do as sacred or secular. The way we live and everything we do can be sacred or holy if our focus is to keep Jesus at the center of it, and our desire is to honor and glorify God and bless others through it.

When my first year at Kelly-Chick & Associates was coming to an end, I asked God what I should do. Should I stay? Should I leave? I saw God at work in our business, as well as in schools in the area, the lacrosse world, and with my friends.

I felt led to stay another year and doubled down on the idea of working hard in whatever I was doing in an effort to honor God and bless and serve others.

THREE LEVELS OF PURPOSE

I decided that if I was going to give the business my best effort, I should look for a group of successful business people who were also passionate about their faith and relationships with God. I wanted to see what I could learn about better integrating my faith and God's Word into our business and into my various roles in the marketplace and community.

It took a few years, but God answered my prayer when He connected me to a group of six men, all business owners, who were involved with an organization called the Christian Business Men's Committee (CBMC). They met for half a day each month to discuss and learn about what God's Word had to say about business, marriage, family, and living on purpose in the marketplace.

Despite my young age (twenty-six at the time), they welcomed me and, over time, helped me come to understand that there are three levels of purpose in life: God's ultimate purpose, God's universal purpose for everyone, and God's unique purpose for each of us as individuals.

Ultimate Purpose

Because God is eternal, all-knowing, all-powerful, and present everywhere, only He knows His ultimate purpose. God reminds us in His Word, "'For my thoughts are not your thoughts, neither are your ways my ways,' declares the Lord. 'As the heavens are higher than the earth, so are my ways higher than your ways and my thoughts than your thoughts.'"[7]

Many things happen in life that we can't explain and do not make sense. Because God gives us free will, and because we are all sinners, not everything that happens is His perfect will or His best for us. Yet, according to God's Word, "...we know that in all things God works for the good of those who love him, who have been called according to His purpose."[8]

Universal Purpose

I also discovered that God wants all of us to understand, embrace, and live out His universal purpose. But He does not force His will on us, even though He leads and desires us to choose His best.

I learned that there are two great parts to God's universal purpose: The Great Commandment and The Great Commission.

In the Gospel of Mark, we read, "One of the teachers of the law came and heard them debating. Noticing that Jesus had given them a good answer, he asked him, 'Of all the commandments, which is the most important?'

'The most important one,' answered Jesus, 'is this: "Hear, O Israel: The Lord our God, the Lord is one. Love the Lord your God with all your heart and with all your soul and with all your mind and with all your strength." The second is this: "Love your neighbor as yourself." There is no commandment greater than these.'"[9]

God's Great Commandment, which is His desire and purpose for all of us, is all about *Love*.

As my friend and former PGA Tour Chaplain, Larry Moody, has shared, "God wants us all to *love* Him completely (with all of our heart, soul, mind, and strength), *love* others compassionately, and *love* ourselves correctly."

The first part of God's universal purpose for all of us is about *love* and relationships: a personal, loving relationship with God; a compassionate, loving relationship with others; and a healthy, loving, truth-based relationship with ourselves.

The second part of God's universal purpose, desire, and hope for all of us is His Great Commission to *Go*.

In the Gospel of Matthew, after Jesus' death and resurrection, Jesus commissioned His followers by telling them to, "Go and make disciples of all nations, baptizing them in the name of the Father and of the Son and of the Holy Spirit, and teaching them to obey everything I have commanded you."[10]

Jesus calls us not only to "come to Him" but to "go for Him" and share His love and truth in word and deed, helping others become disciples and followers of Him.

And Jesus promised the Holy Spirit as a power source, knowing we would need His power if we choose to live out His desired purpose for our lives.

God's universal purpose and desire for each of us is to embrace and live out His Great Commandment (LOVE) and Great Commission (GO). A simple way to summarize this is *"Love & Go,"* and thus the title of this book. Even I can remember that!

In the first part of this book, the focus has been about *Love*. In this second part of the book, there is an emphasis on *Go*. Yet, ultimately, *love* and *go* are integrated and connected when it comes to God's universal purpose.

Unique Purpose

Each of us also has a unique purpose in how we might be a part of God's Great Commandment and Great Commission based on our backgrounds, dispositions, temperaments, life experiences, natural skills, abilities, and spiritual gifts. God has created each of us to play a unique role on His team—if we choose to play it.

One of my favorite books on the topic of purpose is Rick Warren's *The Purpose Driven Life*, which happens to be one of the all-time bestselling books in history, next to the Bible.

In it, Warren uses the acronym *SHAPE* to help us better understand our unique purpose, which includes our *Spiritual gifts, Heart, Abilities, Personality, and Experiences*.[11]

These five things help make you *you* and make me *me*. As we look at each of these areas, we can better understand what God wants to do with each of our individual lives:

- *Spiritual gifts* are God-empowered abilities for serving Him that are given to those who receive, believe, and follow Jesus. These gifts motivate believers for ministry—like serving, teaching, encouraging, leading, giving, sharing the Good News, or offering biblical insight.

- *Heart* refers to the deep desires, hopes, interests, passions, ambitions, dreams, and affections that you and I each uniquely have. It's what we love to do and care about most.

- *Abilities* are the natural talents you and I were born with. God wants us to use our unique, God-given talents and abilities to make the world a better place.

- *Personality* impacts how, why, and where we use our gifts and abilities, and it shapes how we approach life in ways that are different from anyone else.

- *Experiences* teach us practical lessons that shape the way we think and help us mature. They also give us empathy and understanding to help others who are going through similar experiences.

It is amazing that when God made you and me, He broke the mold. There never has been, nor will there ever be, another person created with the same *SHAPE* as you or me.

The hope is that we each find joy, freedom, and renewed energy as we live out the Great Commandment and Great Commission according to our *SHAPE* and unique purpose. God has created and shaped each of us in a specific way for a specific purpose that only you or I can fulfill.

It's true that God gave you a fingerprint that no one else has, so you can leave an imprint that no one else can.

The prophet Jeremiah reminds us that God says, "Before I shaped you in the womb, I knew all about you. Before you saw the light of day, I had holy plans for you."[12]

God's plans for our lives didn't start the moment we were born. His plans started before our birth. The Bible tells us that God shaped you and me in our mother's womb.[13]

The way God shaped each one of us often reveals His unique purpose for our lives and how He wants to use us in His great plan of love and redemption.

We can rest in the truth that God is at work in our lives, and He has shaped each of us to succeed and be effective to *love* and *go* in unique and powerful ways.

God reminds us that He shaped us in advance for these purposes when the Apostle Paul wrote to the church in Ephesus, "For we are God's handiwork, created in Christ Jesus to do good works, which God prepared in advance for us to do."[14]

Rick Warren writes, "God created everybody, God loves everybody, God has a purpose for everybody. But according to God's Word, we must choose to believe and receive Him and His plan in order to fully live out the purpose for which He created us."[15]

Business by the Book—Put it in Writing

In 1991, our CBMC group decided to attend a two-day conference called *Business by the Book* by Larry Burkett. I brought my dad, and we learned so much about what God's Word has to say about business—from hiring to firing, borrowing and lending, investment, and compensation or pay decisions. I also left the conference with a clear understanding of the importance of having both a written personal mission statement and a business mission statement.

The conference speakers told us, "If you aim at nothing, you will hit it every time." I was convinced it would be worth the effort to refocus my life and our business on a mission and purpose that had eternal value and significance.

When I got home, I evaluated other corporate mission statements from companies I respected and further learned how important written mission statements can be to living on purpose.

I wrote a corporate mission/purpose statement and presented it to my dad and brothers. They didn't show much interest and said, "That's fine, whatever!" So, it was really *my* corporate mission/purpose statement for our company—until we were challenged a few years later by a family business consultant to go away as a family and come back with a written mission/purpose that we would all embrace and use as a "North Star" guide for what we desired our business to be. We took the advice and came up with a revised statement that today begins with: "Kelly Benefits is an organization committed to the pursuit of excellence, in an effort to bring honor and glory to God..."

To this day, it hangs on the wall as you enter our corporate headquarters, and we reference it regularly, including in our *Kelly Benefits Culture Guide* and *Kelly Benefits Ambassador Guide*. It has truly focused and reminded us of what is most important. Since dedicating our business and its mission to God's glory and honor, our business has grown more than twenty times in size.

I also wrote a personal mission/purpose statement and have tweaked it over the years. The long version currently reads: "To know and love God and help connect others to Him, His love, His truth, and abundant life in Jesus Christ, through my leadership, relationships, and resources."

Although I am not a full-time professional missionary or church worker, I am a full-time follower of and ambassador for Jesus. I strongly believe that living for God's purposes abundantly blesses our lives on earth and our eternal impact and destiny forever.

In *The Purpose Driven Life*, Rick Warren challenges us to remember, "Life is not about you or me! We exist for God's purposes, not vice versa. We were made by God and for God, and until we understand and embrace that, life will never make sense. When God created us, He gave us a heart and placed in us passions, desires, and dreams, but unless they are under His control, we will often misuse or abuse them or let them lie dormant and waste them. We'll spend sixty, eighty, or one hundred years on earth if we are fortunate to live that long. Yet we'll spend trillions of years in eternity with God in Heaven. Jesus modeled a purpose-driven life, and He taught others how to live for God's purposes as well."[16]

I know I don't want to misuse, abuse, or waste the gifts God has given me. I want to live on purpose and fulfill the dreams and passions God created me to walk in. I believe the only way we can effectively do that is to plug into His Word, His power, and His purpose. God calls each of us not only to live out His purposes but to help others do the same.

LIVING ON PURPOSE

It's been more than thirty-five years since I began working at what is now called Kelly Benefits, started an FCA Huddle at Calvert Hall, began coaching, playing, and growing the influence of FCA in the lacrosse community, and started a number of Bible studies and fellowship groups for many friends and associates.

I'm still on an annual renewable contract with Kelly Benefits and ask God the same question every August about whether I should stay or leave. As of this writing, we have nearly 500 employees serving more than 10,000 corporate clients in the group insurance, benefits, payroll, and HR space. When I first started in the business, we had about a dozen employees and several hundred clients.

The FCA Huddle at Calvert Hall continues to meet each Thursday at 7:30 a.m. in room 108. Today, there are FCA Huddles in more than 300 schools in the state of Maryland, and we have more than ninety full-time FCA staff, serving coaches and athletes through out our state. When I first got involved with FCA as a volunteer in 1987, there were no FCA staff in Maryland, and I didn't know people could join FCA staff.

In addition to staff serving Maryland, there are also more than a dozen FCA Lacrosse staff around the country and the world, including full-time staff in Ukraine, Kenya, Uganda, and Singapore. Every year, thousands of lacrosse players and coaches are being impacted by FCA Lacrosse teams, camps, and convention outreaches.

Many of my childhood friends and others that I have met over time are now leading the Bible studies and fellowship groups that are helping others come to know and grow in their relationship with God.

The book of Proverbs reminds us, "Many are the plans in a person's heart, but it is the Lord's purpose that prevails."[17]

When God said, *Jerusalem, Business, School, Lacrosse,* and *Friends,* I had no idea what He meant. I am so thankful He has allowed me to be a small part of His plan and purpose.

In the context of time, there is no greater way to go than to invest in God, His Word, and the souls of men and women.

How about you? Are you ready to *love* and *go* and live out your unique purpose?

SUGGESTED PRAYER

Dear God,

I believe You created me for a unique purpose. Please help me love You completely, love others compassionately, and love myself correctly. Please help me use the spiritual gifts, heart, abilities, personality, and experiences that You have given me to share Your love and truth with others in both word and deed. Thank You for providing me with an opportunity to love and go as a part of Your eternal plan and purpose. In Jesus' name. Amen.

The Power of Purpose

TRUTH #7:

**God has a unique purpose for you
and living for His purpose will abundantly bless your life
on earth and your eternal destiny forever.**

QUESTIONS FOR REFLECTION

1. When you think of the words *purpose* and *mission*, what comes to mind?

2. What are your thoughts about God's ultimate purpose and the scripture, "'For my thoughts are not your thoughts, neither are your ways my ways,' declares the Lord. 'As the heavens are higher than the earth, so are my ways higher than your ways and my thoughts than your thoughts.'"?

3. Do you believe God's universal purpose for all people is *Love* (love God completely, love others compassionately, love yourself correctly) and *Go* (make disciples by sharing God's love and truth in word and deed)? Why or why not?

4. What do you think about the acronym *SHAPE* (*Spiritual gifts, Heart, Abilities, Personality, Experiences*) to describe a person's unique purpose? What is your understanding of your unique purpose in life?

5. Do you believe God, God's Word, and the souls of men and women are eternal and last forever? How would or should that influence your life?

6. When you think about living an integrated life, what comes to mind?

CHAPTER 8

The Power of Giving

TRUTH #8:

**It is more blessed to give than to receive,
yet God is so generous that you can never outgive Him.**

*"Give, and it will be given to you. A good measure, pressed down,
shaken together and running over, will be poured into your lap.
For with the measure you use, it will be measured to you."*[1]

Jesus

After a week of orientation in Tokyo with hundreds of other U.S. college students, I was sent with a group of about fifty others to Okinawa to teach English, build relationships, and look for opportunities to share God's love and truth with university students. When we weren't tutoring students in English, we were playing basketball and other games with them during their free time.

One of the guys named Scott in our group was a rising junior at Virginia Tech. One day, I noticed his shirt and mentioned how much I liked it. We were about the same size, and the next day, he handed the shirt to me, cleaned and folded, and said, "I want you to have this." A few days later, I saw him do the same thing with his sunglasses. After someone commented on how cool they looked, he took them off his head and gave them to the guy.

I couldn't help but ask him why he was giving away all of his nice stuff. He explained that he had decided to make a verse in the Gospel of Luke his theme for the summer, and he challenged me and the others in our group to memorize it. I had not memorized many Bible verses before, but his example inspired me to do it. After all, I could remember football plays, lacrosse scouting reports, and the information I needed to pass exams—so why not some from Scripture?

The verse captured the words of Jesus in the Gospel of Luke when He said, "Give, and it will be given to you. A good measure, pressed down, shaken together and running over, will be poured into your lap. For with the measure you use, it will be measured to you."[2]

By the end of the summer, I had memorized that verse. Little did I know how much it would shape my thinking about giving for decades to come.

THE SIX T'S OF GIVING

The Bible is full of statements that seem contradictory, like Jesus' words in the Gospel of Luke to "give and it will be given to you,"[3] and the Apostle Paul's reminder to the early church in Ephesus of Jesus' words, "It is more blessed to give than to receive."[4]

How can giving things away be better than receiving them? Does giving always result in blessing in return? And why would Jesus encourage us to give in His name when He doesn't really need anything from us to begin with?

Over the years, I have heard people say, "You can't outgive God."

I appreciate the words of R.G. LeTourneau, the generous industrialist who developed earth-moving machinery, when he wrote about giving: "I shovel out, and God shovels it back . . . but God has a bigger shovel!" I've learned that God's generosity comes back in ways that amaze and affirm His Word.

With this in mind, I have come to believe in and practice what I now call the Six T's of Giving. Those Six T's—*Treasure, Time, Talent, Testimony, Truth,* and *Thanks*—have become a framework for how I try to live my life.

God has been so generous and kind to my family and me, and I now know that when we give and are generous, we are being more like God.

I realize we will never be as giving or generous as God, who gave His only son, Jesus, to literally die so that our sins could be cleansed and forgiven.

One of the most famous verses in the Bible, John 3:16, tells us, "For God so loved the world He gave His one and only Son, that whoever believes in Him shall not perish but have eternal life."

"God so loved . . . He gave." When we give, we express love and faith by giving back some of the resources God has so graciously entrusted to us.

As you read about the Six T's, remember that God's Word confirms that whatever you give away, He will bless and multiply back to you in return—not always in the way you expect it, but always in a way that affirms His goodness, grace, and generosity.

Treasure

There are more than 2,300 verses in the Bible about money and possessions, and it is a subject Jesus often spoke about because He knew that "...where your treasure is, there your heart will be also..."[5]

When we think about treasure and wealth, we usually think of money, financial resources, and material possessions. Since God's Word, the Bible, has so much to say about it, I thought I would share a few scriptures that speak clearly to the issue at hand and have greatly influenced my life.

In Proverbs, King Solomon wrote, "Honor the Lord with your wealth, with the first fruits of all your crops; then your barns will be filled to overflowing, and your vats will brim over with new wine."[6]

Solomon, King David's son, is considered by many to be one of the wisest and wealthiest people who ever lived. In this proverb, he was trying to impart some basic truths and principles to his son when he wrote about the importance of honoring the Lord with "first fruits."

In this scenario and time in history, the interpretation is somewhat literal. Solomon lived in an agricultural society where wealth or material well-being was often tied to the ability to produce livestock or crops from the land. Solomon challenged his son—and now challenges us through these inspired words—to give our best to God, or our first fruits, and not what is left over.

Many people, even Christians, will give to the Lord's work or special causes if they have anything left over at the end of the month. But God's desire, and His best for us, is to recognize that His causes and our giving need to be the first line item on our budget.

The challenge is to be a first-fruits giver as a way to prioritize our relationship with Him, express thankfulness, and demonstrate faith in His continued provision.

God tells us that if we give our best and first fruits for His glory and the good of others, our barns (lives) will be filled to overflowing, and our vats (hearts) will brim over with new wine. He may not bless us with financial or material gifts, but He promises a full and overflowing life, which is symbolic of Jesus and the Holy Spirit—the sources of abundant life, joy, peace, hope, faith, and love, which are gifts you cannot buy, and the world can never give.

Rick Warren writes, "Don't give God your leftovers. When you choose instead to give Him the first of everything you have, God promises to give you everything you need—and more."[7]

Another compelling scripture on giving was penned by the Holy Spirit, through the prophet Malachi, who wrote, "Bring the whole tithe into the storehouse, that there may be food in my house. Test me in this," says the Lord Almighty, "and see if I will not throw open the floodgates of heaven and pour out so much blessing that there will not be room enough to store it."[8]

This scripture is the only place in the Bible where the Lord says, "test me in this"—with a promise to "throw open the floodgates of heaven and pour out so much blessing that you will not have room enough for it."

Wow! But still, so many of us don't want to trust the Lord by giving generously—at least the first 10 percent of what He has entrusted to us. After all, God owns it all anyway, and He does not need our money. In many ways, He tells us to give so that we might be blessed.

God reminds us in the Psalms that "every animal of the forest is mine, and the cattle on a thousand hills. I know every bird in the mountains, and the insects in the fields are mine."[9] God owns it all, yet He is so gracious that He only asks us to give a small percentage of what He has so generously given us back to Him and to others in need.

Some would say that since the time of Jesus' life, death, and resurrection, we are no longer bound by the Old Testament law of tithing found in Proverbs and Malachi. Yet, in a letter to the newly formed church in Corinth (modern-day Greece), the Apostle Paul wrote, "Each of you should give what you have decided in your heart to give, not reluctantly or under compulsion, for God loves a cheerful giver."[10]

At the end of the day, we don't *have* to give. We *get* to give! God's economy is different, as He graciously lets us be a part of His loving, just, merciful, and redemptive work here on earth.

God wants us to be cheerful, generous givers, so in my mind, a tithe (or 10 percent) is a minimum. And from an investment perspective, since God promises such a generous return and eternal reward, including treasure in heaven, we are wise to give or invest generously.

In the Gospel of Matthew, Jesus challenges His followers, "Do not store up for yourselves treasures on earth, where moth and rust destroy, and where thieves break in and steal. But store up for yourselves treasures in heaven, where neither moth nor rust destroys, and where thieves do not break in or steal."[11]

Randy Alcorn, in his book *The Treasure Principle*, writes, "If we give instead of keep, if we invest in the eternal—instead of the temporal, we store up treasure in heaven that will never stop paying dividends. Whatever treasures we store up on earth will be left behind when we leave. Whatever treasures we store up in heaven will be waiting for us when we arrive."[12]

Clearly, how we live and give today will impact our eternal existence forever.

I appreciate the story of Sir John Templeton, a highly regarded banker and investor who was recognized in the 1990s by *Money* magazine as arguably the greatest stock picker of the twentieth century. I have heard it said that when he spoke to a class at Harvard Business School, a student asked him, "Sir, if there was one piece of investment advice you would give us above any other, what would it be?" Templeton immediately replied, "Oh, that's easy. Give at least the first 10 percent of everything you make to the work of the Lord." Over his lifetime, Templeton gave away over $1 billion to charitable causes.

Our Tithing Journey

Some say you shouldn't consider tithing or giving away money until you reach a certain income level. All I can tell you is that since Gayle and I have been married, we have tried to give at least 10 percent, as we have understood it. When we married in 1987, I made $25,000 a year, and Gayle made $11,000 as a schoolteacher. That's $36,000 total, which meant our tithe was about $3,600 a year, or $300 per month.

We learned that there are four types of givers: non-givers, reluctant givers, dutiful givers, and joyful givers. When we started our giving journey, I would say we were somewhat reluctant, dutiful givers, but we decided we wanted to obey God's Word, invest in eternity, and tithe from the first day of our marriage. And boy, has God blessed us!

Because we started early and made our tithe the first line item on our budget, we have never questioned our practice of giving and have been blessed in so many ways by it. Today, we experience great joy in our giving, and we have fun making most of our giving decisions together.

We ultimately set up a separate checking account we call our "tithe account." Every payday, our budgeted amount is deposited directly into our tithe account, and the rest into our normal checking and savings or investment accounts. That makes it easy and enjoyable to give away money.

A number of years ago, we also opened a donor-advised fund (DAF) in our family's name through an organization called the National Christian Foundation. This allows us to make tax-deductible contributions into our own family-controlled charitable fund that we can give away when we are ready or feel led. There are no fund minimums or administrative or regulatory hassles, so almost anyone can set up a DAF. With our fund, I don't generally like to let money sit in there too long because I like to give it as we get it. That money burns a hole in my pocket because it's so much fun to give as the Lord graciously gives to us.

I also like the wisdom of what some call the "10-10-80 rule" as it applies to your weekly, monthly, and annual income: Give 10 percent, save 10 percent, and live off the remaining 80 percent.

People often ask, "Should I give 10 percent of my gross income or net income after taxes?" Seek the Lord, and He will lead you. Either way, you'll see God's blessings at work, and He will give you joy and cheer you on as you trust Him with the money and treasure that He has entrusted to you. As a reminder, you don't give to get, but when you give, you get! It's God's law of sowing and reaping.

Today, Gayle and I are blessed to give away more each year than we ever dreamed we would even earn. I don't say this to brag in any way, but only to give God the glory for His generosity and to marvel at His goodness.

In His famous Sermon on the Mount, Jesus said many powerful things, including, "...when you give to the needy, do not let your left hand know what your right hand is doing, so that your giving may be in secret. Then your Father, who sees what is done in secret, will reward you."[13]

In general, Gayle and I don't want to draw attention to our giving, which is relatively small in light of God's economy. We just want to draw attention to God's goodness, grace, and generosity in our lives. We are so grateful He lets us be a part of His love, grace, and redemptive plan for others.

After all, the only person Jesus shouts out as a generous giver in all the scriptures is a poor widow who put two pennies into the offering basket.[14] She gave more than those who put in thousands, even millions, of dollars because she literally gave everything she had.

When we give, our desire is to obey, honor, and trust God and His provision, bless people in need, and invest in things that will last forever.

God Owns It All

After Gayle and I got married, we rented a small tenant house (about 800 square feet) on the back of a ten-acre farm. By agreeing to mow their lawn and fields each week, the owner only charged us $200 a month.

A year later, we nervously bought our first home, an 1,800 square-foot townhouse, and we loved the ten years we lived there. We were able to host many neighborhood events and Bible studies, and allow various people to live with us during times of need.

As our family grew, God opened a door for us to design and have a larger house built in a beautiful new neighborhood and a great location. This created opportunities for us to host even larger groups for sports teams that I coached, various Bible studies and fellowship groups we led, and guests we housed.

After twenty years in our home, I reluctantly agreed to an addition of a great room and expanded kitchen that Gayle envisioned, and I am very glad I did. Today, we are able to host even more people in our home, always with a desire to be a light and witness to the goodness and glory of God.

We have let many people use our home to host bridal and baby showers, retirement parties, and even baptisms in our backyard pool. And every summer, we have up to five or six FCA interns and/or missionaries living in our basement. We sincerely believe God owns our house and all of our possessions, and we are merely stewards or managers of them.

Today, we are blessed to also own homes in Fenwick Island, Delaware, and Vero Beach, Florida. These vacation homes have allowed us to host and house many family members, friends, and ministry leaders.

There is no promise or guarantee from God that we will always own a nice house or homes in beautiful places. But while we do, our desire is for them to be bright lights for God's glory and places where people come to know, grow, and rest in Him.

After all, God owns everything He has blessed and entrusted us with, and we desire to manage and steward those resources with wisdom, grace, and generosity. And that includes our business, Kelly Benefits, where, as a family, we are thankful for opportunities to sponsor and give to organizations serving those in need.

We also love it when various groups and nonprofit organizations that align with our mission and values use one of our corporate headquarters' twelve conference rooms or Education Center that can seat more than one hundred people. It is so cool when I walk through our offices and see several nonprofit and faith-based organizations advancing their cause and using the office facilities God has entrusted to us.

Priority, Plan, Percentage...

Gayle and I attend a church in Lutherville, Maryland, called Church of the Nativity. The leaders often talk about making giving a *priority,* having a giving *plan,* choosing to give a *percentage* of your earnings (even if you start at 1 or 2 percent), considering a *progressive* increase in your giving each year as God continues to bless you, and *praying* about how God wants you and your family to give going forward.

I marvel at the story of William Colgate, the founder of Colgate® Toothpaste and the Colgate-Palmolive Company. He was born in England, and his family emigrated to Baltimore, Maryland, when he was fifteen years old. He had very little money, but it is my understanding that he started his business career as a 10 percent tither and progressively increased his giving so that, by the end of his career and life, he gave away 90 percent and kept 10 percent—or what I call a reverse-tither.

I am no William Colgate, but Gayle and I have purposed to progressively increase the percentage of what we give each year from what God has so graciously given to us.

Another fun story is about my good friend Ed Bradley. We met more than thirty years ago at a Baltimore Orioles game. A few days later, he reached out about getting together to discuss life and faith. It led us to go through a discipleship program called Operation Timothy, where we studied the biblical principles of tithing, and he began to apply biblical truths to his giving.

He often jokes with me that our friendship has cost him more money than any other. He even ended up retiring from his big corporate job at the age of fifty-two to go on full-time staff at his church. I often prod him back by asking about his life and God's amazing provision since he began applying God's Word to his giving. He can only smile, laugh, and nod with approval.

God's blessings and provision are amazing. You can't outgive Him!

Time

For many of us, as we get older, it is easier to cut a check or give away some treasure than it is to give of our time. After all, time is a finite resource, and we are all given the same number of minutes in a day, days in a week, weeks in a month, and months in a year. No amount of money can buy us more time.

God's Word challenges us to use our time wisely.

In what is considered to be the oldest of the 150 Psalms in the Bible, Moses wrote, "Teach us to number our days, that we may gain a heart of wisdom."[15]

The Holy Spirit, through Moses, also wrote in that same Psalm, "Our days may come to seventy years, or eighty, if our strength endures..."[16]

As I mentioned in the Introduction, in 2024, I turned sixty. That sounded old to me at the time. For some reason, when I hit that age, I began counting how many years I might have left on this earth.

I believe each of our days is numbered. As King David wrote in Psalm 139, "All the days ordained for me were written in Your book before one of them came to be."[17]

So, only God knows how many days, weeks, months, or years we have to live. For illustration's sake, let's assume I live to be eighty. That would mean, at the time of this writing, I have about twenty years—or 240 months, or 1,040 weeks, or 7,305 days (I think I might be taking this numbering thing too seriously)—left to live.

And the Apostle Paul reminds us, "Therefore be careful how you walk, not as unwise men, but as wise, making the most of your time..."[18]

The point remains that whatever we choose to give our time to consumes one of our most valuable resources, and as my friend and author Todd Hopkins says, "God has the ability to expand our effective use of time."

I flash back to the fraternity/sorority Bible study at Cornell. As soon as I started attending, it always seemed that I ended up with a major assignment or exam the day after we met. I often thought I should skip Bible study to finish my work or study for the exam. But I learned that if I put God and His Word first, He often blessed the time that I did prepare, and I got more done in less time than usual.

Today, we like to provide the people who work in our family business the flexibility and opportunity to use some of their work time to volunteer for organizations and causes that honor God and bless and serve people in need. It's amazing how effective and fruitful these folks are in the work they do at Kelly Benefits and in the community.

When we give our time and presence to an organization, a cause, or a person in need, I believe God often blesses or multiplies the effectiveness of our time that remains. Only He knows how much time on this earth we each have left, so we need to use it and give it wisely.

Talent

Our talent, like our time, is also a limited resource (definitely in my case). God gives us different talents and abilities, and how we share and use our talents to honor God and bless others is of great importance.

Jesus told a parable, recorded in the Gospels of Matthew and Luke, about different talents that were given to three people. One was given five talents, another two talents, and a third, one talent. The ones who were given multiple talents invested those talents wisely, doubled (or increased) their talents, and were ultimately given more. The person with one talent buried it and ended up having that one talent taken from them.[19]

God does not judge those in the parable—or us—by what we have, but by what we do with what we have. We are each called to use our talents so that they increase and ultimately bless and serve others.

In my experience, when we share our talents, skills, and abilities to bless, help, and serve others, God often blesses and expands our talents and influence. And in regard to His Church, God gives each of us different gifts, ultimately to share, bless, and serve others in the Body of Christ—and vice versa.

And outside the church, I think back to when I was coaching the faceoff men on the Calvert Hall lacrosse team. It was fun working with high school athletes, and even though I was working full-time in our family business, when I gave my time and talent to help those young faceoff athletes improve their technique, skill, and ability, I saw my own faceoff talent, skill, and ability improve as well. I ended up playing high-level lacrosse, including professional indoor lacrosse, getting invited to multiple U.S. National Team tryouts, and being recognized as one of the top faceoff athletes and coaches in the country during that time.

As I shared my talents and skills with others, I believe God blessed and multiplied my talents and skills. Many of the athletes I coached came to our FCA Huddle, as I had earned their trust, and many of them entered into and grew in their relationship with God.

The same principle applies when we share a business, academic, artistic, or other type of skill or talent. Many times, what we receive in return expands our gifting, talent, and platform of influence—all for God's glory.

Testimony

A testimony is defined as a formal, written, or spoken statement about an experience or a public recounting of a religious conversion or experience. I like to say that a testimony, from a spiritual sense anyway, is someone's personal faith story or how someone became a follower of Jesus.

Everyone has a unique and beautiful story in God's eyes. God has purposely blessed each of us with a different story that we should be prepared to share when the right opportunities arise. It might be a one-on-one conversation, a conversation over a meal with a small number of people, or a time of sharing before a larger group seeking perspective and insight on the deeper questions of life.

I believe and have experienced that when we share or give away our testimony or personal faith story, God often blesses and expands our testimony, as well as the number of people it reaches and influences. A personal testimony or faith story usually includes three parts:

1. What our life was like before we entered into a personal relationship with God.
2. What happened and how we came to believe, receive, and trust Jesus as our Savior and Lord.
3. What our lives have been like since we decided to surrender to and follow Him.

Although it might be uncomfortable at first, we ultimately receive many benefits when we share our testimony or personal faith story. These include reminding ourselves of God's goodness, grace, mercy, and blessings in our lives. Also, we never fully know what is going on in the lives of others who might be listening and how our story might bless and encourage their hearts, minds, and story in ways we could never imagine.

Our job is to faithfully share our story and God's truth, be a witness to God's goodness in our lives, and believe that God will work in others' lives. Only God can open eyes, ears, hearts, and minds, so we must trust Him for the outcome.

The Apostle Peter challenged all followers of Jesus when he wrote, "...Always be prepared to give an answer to everyone who asks you to give the reason for the hope that you have..."[20]

We need to be prepared to share our personal testimony and faith story, the truth and good news of the Gospel, and the hope that we have as the Lord opens doors. As we give away our story, we trust God to bless other people's stories with the ultimate hope of honoring God and His story.

Speaking of stories, I love the story of the Apostles Peter and John in the book of Acts when they are confronted by a man who had been crippled from birth, sitting at the temple gate and begging for money. Apparently, he was carried to the temple gate regularly and received enough money from passersby to survive.

But the day he met Peter and John and heard the testimonies of their experience with Jesus, the crippled man received something much greater than money. When the man cried out for help, "...Peter said, 'Silver or gold I do not have, but what I do have I give you. In the name of Jesus Christ of Nazareth, walk.' Taking him by the right hand, he helped him up, and instantly the man's feet and ankles became strong. He jumped to his feet and began to walk..."[21]

Peter and John had no financial treasure to give, but in Jesus' name, they shared a testimony and truth that gave the man new life, new legs, and new hope.

The power of a testimony or an encounter with Jesus can never be discounted. Many times, it's easier to give money than the gift of our time and testimony. Yet, in so many situations, a testimony of God's goodness and truth is the greatest gift.

Truth

Jesus said, "I am the way and the truth and the life. No one comes to the Father except through me."[22] He also said, "If you hold to my teaching, you are really my disciples. Then you will know the truth, and the truth will set you free."[23]

The truth is powerful, life-changing, the way to the Father, and a path to freedom. That is why I like to share it—or give it away—so others might be blessed by it as well. There are so many ways we can share God's truth, even if we don't fully understand it ourselves or know how to articulate it perfectly.

I appreciate the story of Andrew and his brother Peter in the Gospel of John. Andrew had already become a believer in Jesus when he came to his brother Simon (whom Jesus later renamed Peter) and told him, "'We have found the Messiah,' [that is, the Christ]. And he brought him to Jesus."[24]

Andrew didn't have all the answers and probably couldn't articulate or explain his new faith very well, but he gave his brother a gift and blessing by bringing him to the source of truth, to see and decide for himself.

Like Andrew, you don't have to have all the answers to help connect others to the truth. Over the years, I have found different ways to give away or share the truth, even if I can't explain it properly or in a timely manner. At the office, I have stocked what I call my "truth closet" with my favorite books and resources that I can proactively give to others as the Spirit leads.

When you give away a well-written book or devotional, direct someone to an interesting podcast or video series, or extend a simple invitation to a church service, small group, seminar, or retreat that proclaims the truth in a practical and relevant way, you are giving truth. And when we give away truth, I believe the Lord often expands the truth that we are all able to comprehend, embrace, and receive.

A favorite way we like to give away truth through our business is by providing all of our employees access to a Family Life Weekend to Remember marriage and parenting conference. We cover the registration and hotel costs, and many of our people come back from that weekend thanking us for the time they had and the truth and perspective they learned, which blessed and, in some cases, saved their marriages.

Another favorite employee benefit we provide is scholarships to a variety of faith-based summer camps for the children of our employees. We pay most of the camp costs, and for the children who attend, they are blessed to see, hear, and experience the truth of God's love, grace, and Word.

God demonstrates His grace and generosity to us when He enlightens us to His truth, and we are truly blessed when we give away or share His truth with others.

Thanks

Giving thanks to God is probably my favorite "T," and the easiest of the Six T's to give away. I think it is easy to give thanks to God because you can do it any time and any place.

It does not have to be out loud or visible to others. It does not have to be in a church or religious setting, and it doesn't have to be on a holiday or at a meal. You can do it quietly in your heart and mind or out loud whenever and wherever you choose.

And we know for sure it's God's will for us to give Him thanks by reading the Apostle Paul's letter to the Thessalonians, where he wrote, "...give thanks in all circumstances; for this is God's will for you in Christ Jesus."[25]

I'm challenged by a story in the Gospel of Luke about Jesus being confronted by ten men who had the highly contagious and infectious disease of leprosy. These men were quarantined and not allowed to interact with others. From a distance, they shouted, "Jesus, Master, have pity on us!"[26]

Jesus told them to go see the priests in their town, and as they went, they were cleansed and miraculously healed. One of them, when he saw that he was healed, came back, praising God in a loud voice. He threw himself at Jesus' feet and thanked Him. Jesus asked, "Where are the other nine? Has no one returned to give praise to God except this foreigner?"[27]

It's hard to believe the nine other lepers who were healed did not come back to thank Jesus, but it makes me think of the times I forget to thank Him for the many blessings He has bestowed on my family and me.

I love the way the one leper came back to Jesus—not only to thank Him but to do so sincerely and passionately by literally falling to his knees and bowing before Him.

How we choose to give thanks to the Lord, we just need to remember and have the humility to do it.

I have found that an easy way to give God thanks is through Christian music. Many faith-based songs are essentially "thank you" ballads to the Lord. When we sing those words of praise and thanks, we are blessing the God we love. And I believe the more thanks we give God, the more He gives us for which to be thankful.

TWO SEAS

In the summer of 2018, the Men's World Lacrosse Championships were held in Netanya, Israel. We took a team through FCA Lacrosse, which we called Team Serve, to go and help World Lacrosse and the Israel Lacrosse Association in any way we could. As volunteers, we also hoped to practice with and serve as many of the forty-six countries that were there to compete as we could.

Over the two weeks we were there to serve, we were also able to do some sightseeing. One day, we made our way to the world-famous Dead Sea, which lies more than 430 feet below sea level.

After swimming (or really, floating, because of the extreme saltiness of the water) in the Dead Sea, I took a minute to pull our group together and remind everyone that the water in the Dead Sea is nearly ten times saltier than the ocean. The salinity of the water is so high that plants and animals cannot live or flourish there, hence its name. I also pointed out that the water in the Dead Sea actually comes from the beautiful Sea of Galilee, where Jesus spent a lot of time (and where we had visited and swam earlier in the week), and where His disciples often fished in the fresh, clean water that was teeming with life.

I explained that the Jordan River, where Jesus was baptized, flows down from the mountains into the top, or north, end of the Sea of Galilee (which is really more like a freshwater lake than a sea). It then runs out the bottom, or south, end of the Sea of Galilee for another 104 winding miles into the Dead Sea, which has no outlet. The water flows into the Dead Sea and stays there, stagnating and ultimately eliminating all life within it.

It was a powerful reminder that if we receive without giving, we'll stagnate like the Dead Sea, and nothing good will grow in or around us. Whatever God allows to flow into our lives—whether it's *Treasure, Time, Talent, Testimony, Truth,* or *Thanks*—God desires for some of it to flow out of our lives to bless and serve others.

St. Francis of Assisi, the Italian mystic, poet, and Catholic friar who founded the religious order of the Franciscans, wrote in the early 1200s, "Remember that when you leave this earth, you can take nothing that you have received with you, but only what you have given."

The Apostle Paul, more than a thousand years before St. Francis of Assisi, reminded the early church in Corinth of Jesus' words when He said, "...whoever sows generously will also reap generously."[28]

Nearly 1,000 years before the Apostle Paul, King Solomon penned the Proverb that says, "One person gives freely, yet gains even more; another withholds unduly, but comes to poverty. A generous person will prosper; whoever refreshes others will be refreshed."[29]

And today, Rick Warren reminds us, "Every time you give, your heart grows bigger, you grow spiritually, and you break the grip of materialism in your life."[30]

When we give our *Treasure, Time, Talent, Testimony, Truth,* and *Thanks,* we are being generous like God and it is a way to *Go* and win a spiritual victory every time.

Since truth is eternal and I can't outgive God, I want His blessings in my life to flow through me to bless others and have an eternal impact. One way I want to *love* and *go* is by being a generous giver, sower, and investor in God's kingdom.

How about you?

SUGGESTED PRAYER

Dear God,

Thank You for Your incredible generosity! Thank You for giving me access to abundant life and eternal life through the gift of Your Son, Jesus. Please help me grow in the giving away of the treasure, time, talent, testimony, truth, and thanks that You have so graciously entrusted to me. Thank You for Your promises throughout Your Word that confirm that I cannot outgive You. Help me love and go to be a generous giver like You.

In Jesus' name. Amen.

The Power of Giving

TRUTH #8:

It is more blessed to give than to receive,

yet God is so generous that you can never outgive Him.

QUESTIONS FOR REFLECTION

1. What strikes you about Jesus' words when He says, "Give and it will be given to you. A good measure, pressed down, shaken together and running over, will be poured into your lap. For with the measure you use, it will be measured to you"?

2. When you consider the Six T's of Giving, which T—Treasure, Time, Talent, Testimony, Truth, or Thanks—is the easiest and most fun for you to give? Which is the hardest to give?

3. What do you think about tithing (giving away the first 10 percent of your income) and the idea of priority, plan, percentage, progressive, and prayer as it relates to giving?

4. What was your favorite story about giving or generosity from this chapter? Why?

5. Who is someone in your life who has modeled generosity and giving?

6. Is there a giving goal or two you would like to establish in your life? Explain.

The Power of Relationships and Community

TRUTH #9:

There is nothing more important in life than relationships and the best way to grow in your relationship with God, others, and even yourself, is in community.

"And let us consider how we may spur one another on toward love and good deeds, not giving up meeting together, as some are in the habit of doing."[1]

The Apostle Paul*

I appreciate the African proverb that says, "If you want to go fast, go alone. If you want to go far, go together."

For some reason, God created us to function best when we are in relationship and community with others. Even God models the value of relationships and community, being three persons—Father, Son (Jesus), and Holy Spirit—yet one God. The Trinity, God being three persons in one, is the ultimate example of community. Since we are created in the image of God, we are created to function best in community as well.

Community is all about relationships, and Jesus reminds us that there is nothing more important than our love relationship with God, others, and ourselves. In order to grow and maximize these relationships, we need each other's help.

I have heard it said that we learn and grow more in circles than rows, and I have found that to be true in my own life.

* The letter to the Hebrews does not mention the name of its author but has traditionally been attributed to the Apostle Paul.

For many years, church was simply showing up, sitting in the same pew (or row), and listening (or pretending to listen) to a homily, sermon, or message. It was almost always a one-way communication or monologue by the priest, pastor, or speaker. Most of it went in one ear and out the other as I daydreamed about sports, girls, and whatever else floated through my mind; and thus, I often failed to connect with the message.

During that first fraternity/sorority Bible study I attended at Cornell, I discovered the power of a circle. As eight to ten of us sat in that room, reading and discussing the selected scripture, life, and the challenge of applying God's Word to our lives, I experienced transformation. I learned so much from everyone else's comments and questions as they shared with humility and honesty from their hearts. It was incredible fellowship and true community.

I once heard "true community" defined as a group of people who love and are loved, serve and are served, know and are known, and celebrate and are celebrated. I like to add that true community is also a place where you learn and grow while helping others learn and grow as well.

Over the years, I have been part of many small groups, huddles, and house church gatherings where the fellowship, loving, serving, knowing, celebrating, and learning have been transformational for everyone involved. Yet, even faith-based small groups, teams, and organizations can have their challenges. Because we are human, we all bring our sin nature, baggage, and idiosyncrasies to the table. No small group, team, or organization is perfect, and it's easy to become negative and want to disconnect.

Some of us can bring deep, hidden pain to a group or team. Perhaps things happened to us as children, or even as adults, that were painful and wrong. We are wise to understand that "hurt people, hurt people," and extend grace and assistance where possible.

Although no group, organization, or team is perfect, we should remember the Proverb penned by King Solomon that says, "Where there are no oxen, the manger [or stable] is clean, but abundant crops come by the strength of the ox."[2]

Whenever two or more people gather together, even in the name of the

Lord, there will (as I like to say) be "some poop in the barn." But we are able to learn, grow, and accomplish so much more together than we ever could alone in an empty, clean stable.

One of our enemy's most effective strategies is to isolate and divide us. We are always more vulnerable to attack when we are separated from community, fellowship, and relationships with others.

I can relate to the illustration of a bonfire on the beach. When all of the wood and coals are together, the fire burns brightly and with full power. But if you take a single coal or piece of wood from the burning fire and set it aside by itself for an extended period of time, it loses its power, heat, and energy. Coals need each other to produce their full potential, and so do we as people.

Rick Warren reminds us, "We are created for community, fashioned for fellowship, and formed for a family, and none of us can fulfill God's purposes by ourselves."[3]

God created us to grow, develop, and function best in the context of "one another" relationships. The Apostle Paul wrote that we should "...encourage one another and build each other up..."[4] In fact, there are more than fifty "one another" commands in the Bible that you cannot obey unless you are in community and fellowship with others—from "love one another,"[5] to "pray for one another,"[6] to "comfort one another,"[7] to "forgive one another,"[8] just to name a few.

God has wired us to need connection with others in His family to grow. One of the best ways to do that is through involvement in a local church, ideally one that has small groups.

THE CHURCH IS NOT A BUILDING

My wife Gayle and I love to travel, and one of our favorite countries to visit is Italy. My mom's mother's side of the family immigrated to America in the late 1800s from a small town called Montella, in an area of Italy called Avellino, which is south of Rome and east of Naples.

Montella, like every other town in Italy, has an old church building with a bell tower. It is estimated that there are more than 20,000 Catholic churches in Italy, including some of the largest cathedrals in the world, such as St. Peter's Basilica in Rome, Duomo di Milano in Milan, and Duomo di Firenze in Florence.

When I saw these old churches and cathedrals, I marveled at the incredible dedication and passion of the people who built them. Every stone, statue, and stained-glass window was created with the desire to honor God and provide a house of worship.

Construction on the cathedral in Milan, also known as the Basilica of the Nativity of Saint Mary, began in 1386 and wasn't officially completed until 1965—nearly 600 years later. Talk about dedication and perseverance!

Although I could see the beauty of these old churches, there's also a coldness about them. The problem is, many of these churches today are empty and function more as museums or tourist sites than as places to worship God.

One day, an Italian tour guide showed us some of the well-known but smaller churches in Milan. In one mid-sized church, where no one else was present, we noticed a Bible on a wooden stand in the middle of the aisle leading up to the altar. It was opened to a gospel reading, and we asked our guide if she could translate the passage, which was written in Italian. As she quietly read God's Word to us in English, we were aggressively confronted by a caretaker of the church.

"Be quiet," he said. "You are in church. You are not allowed to talk in a church."

What? Our tour guide was quietly reading God's Word out loud in an empty church, and we were rebuked for it? No wonder so many church buildings sit empty today.

The good news is that the Church of Jesus Christ is not a building, or network of buildings, no matter how beautiful or historic they may be. According to God's Word, the Church is the universal Body of Christ—the family and people of God. Jesus tells us, "For where two or three gather in my name, there am I with them."[9]

Think about it: When you read the Bible, you never hear about church buildings where the believers and followers of Jesus met. In the early church, believers met in each other's homes for fellowship and worship and to learn more about Jesus and His teachings.

For more than twenty years, Gayle and I attended a nondenominational church called Grace Fellowship, which met in a high school gym and then a renovated furniture warehouse. During that time, we were part of numerous small groups, often called "cell groups" or "house churches."

Today, we are thankful to attend an amazing Catholic church called Church of the Nativity. The facility, which can hold up to 1,500 people, is beautiful, and the fellowship and teaching are amazing. The church also supports more than 200 small groups that meet at various times and locations each week. Most groups meet in homes, while some meet virtually online.

We have also spent time in parts of Africa—Uganda, Kenya, Ethiopia, and Ghana—where the local church buildings may not be very impressive, but the community, fellowship, and love are inspiring.

Across the world, church buildings and other facilities—like school gyms, community centers, and other retrofitted spaces—are important for creating places to meet. But at the end of the day, church is less about where you meet and more about a community where you can grow in your relationship with God, others, and even yourself.

Participation in a local church is vital for spiritual growth, community, and fulfilling God's purposes. Rick Warren reminds us, "A Christian without a church is an orphan."[10]

OUR FIRST COMMUNITY

The first community God created for each one of us to experience is our earthly family, beginning with our parents and any siblings in our nuclear family.

In Paul's letter to the Ephesians, we are called to "obey your parents" and to then "honor your father and mother—which is the first commandment with a promise—so that it may go well with you and that you may enjoy long life on the earth."[11]

This same command and promise appear in the Ten Commandments recorded by Moses in the Old Testament book of Exodus.[12] Written more than 1,200 years before Paul's letter to the Ephesians, it must be an eternal truth God wants us to really understand and apply.

My parents are now in their mid-80s, and to this day, I try to honor my mom and dad in both word and deed. I realize that not everyone grows up with both parents or, in some cases, with either parent present. Yet, we are still called to honor our parents or whoever that parental figure is in our lives.

I have three brothers. I am the oldest, followed by my brother John, then David, then Bryan. There are only four and a half years between me and my youngest brother Bryan. For the past thirty-plus years, we have worked together in our family business.

One day, I was complaining to a friend who was strong in his faith and had two brothers and a father with a strong personality.

I said, "Just imagine working every day with your brothers and your father."

He said, "There is no way I could do that. You just described hell to me."

We both laughed, but his comment made me realize how challenging relationships, especially family relationships, can be.

When people ask what it's like to work in a family business with your brothers and other family members, I usually tell them, "For us, nine out of ten days are great." Then I jokingly say, "I just won't tell you about that tenth day."

Most people can relate. Relationships are not easy, even with family, and for some, especially with family.

Have you heard the saying, "Familiarity breeds contempt?" The longer you know someone or spend a lot of time with them, the easier and more likely it becomes to take that person for granted, lose patience, and focus on their faults rather than their strengths. This is especially true within families.

At times, it is wise to engage counselors or advisors who can help navigate family relationships. My brothers and I meet monthly with a spiritual leadership coach and a strategic business advisor. Together, they hold us accountable to live out our Kelly Benefits' Cornerstone, which is

Love, and our Corporate Values of *Integrity, Excellence, Respect, Humility,* and *Generosity.*

God's Word says, "The way of a fool is right in his own eyes, but a wise man is he who listens to counsel."[13] It also says, "Plans fail for lack of counsel, but with many advisors they succeed."[14]

We all have blind spots—individually and corporately. Wise counselors and advisors can help us identify and understand those blind spots so we can more effectively accomplish our individual, family, and business mission and purpose in a way that honors God.

COMMUNITY OF FRIENDS

The Proverbs say, "A friend loves at all times, and a brother is born for a time of adversity."[15]

I am thankful for my brothers. Even though we fought, competed, and battled quite a bit growing up—and still do occasionally as we work together in our business—we know that if any one of us has a personal, family, or business problem, we will be there for each other. That is a blessing of family.

Unfortunately, many people do not have family, or brothers or sisters to support them in times of need. Yet, God often provides spiritual brothers and sisters in Christ, or friends, when we need them most.

One of my favorite stories in the Bible is about a paralyzed man who was brought to Jesus by four of his friends. The story, found in the Gospel of Mark, goes like this:

> A few days later, when Jesus again entered Capernaum, the people heard that he had come home.
>
> They gathered in such large numbers that there was no room left, not even outside the door, and he preached the word to them. Some men came, bringing to him a paralyzed man, carried by four of them. Since they could not get him to Jesus because of the crowd, they made an opening in the roof above Jesus by digging through it and then lowered the mat the man was lying on. When Jesus saw their faith, he said to the paralyzed man, "Son, your sins are forgiven."

> Now some teachers of the law were sitting there, thinking to themselves, "Why does this fellow talk like that? He's blaspheming! Who can forgive sins but God alone?"
>
> Immediately Jesus knew in his spirit that this was what they were thinking in their hearts, and he said to them, "Why are you thinking these things? Which is easier: to say to this paralyzed man, 'Your sins are forgiven,' or to say, 'Get up, take your mat and walk'?
>
> But I want you to know that the Son of Man has authority on earth to forgive sins." So, he said to the man, "I tell you, get up, take your mat and go home."
>
> He got up, took his mat and walked out in full view of them all. This amazed everyone and they praised God, saying, "We have never seen anything like this!"[16]

The paralytic's friends were so persistent and determined to have him meet Jesus that, despite being unable to get into the house because of the huge crowd, they hoisted him onto the roof, dug a hole in the mud-and-thatch roof, and lowered the mat so that he lay right before Jesus.

As the Scripture shows, when Jesus saw the faith of the paralytic's friends, He chose to heal the man spiritually by forgiving his sins and then physically by telling him to get up, take his mat, and walk home, which he did.

In the process, Jesus also proved to the religious leaders, who were hoping to trap and destroy Him, that He was God. After all, only God can forgive sins, and only God can make a paralyzed man walk.

Sometimes in life, we may be so disheartened that we need family or friends to carry us to Jesus for help and healing. Other times, we may be the friend God uses to help carry someone else. God has wired us to need each other. In many cases, we can't get rid of our hurts, habits, or hangups on our own.

Stuck in the Mud

There was a day when I decided to take a shortcut to get to my destination, which took me down a dirt road. It had rained heavily earlier in the day, and although the road was a little muddy, it was drivable, or at least that is what I thought.

My problem began when another car was coming toward me, and I pulled over to let it pass. As I pressed the gas to get back to the center of the road, my back right tire got stuck in the mud and started spinning in place. Being the crazy, Type A personality that I am, I pressed the gas pedal harder, managing to inch the car forward slightly before it settled back in the rut. The more I pressed the gas pedal, the bigger the rut became. Eventually, I had to call a couple of friends who brought a piece of plywood to place under my tire for traction. With each of them pushing, I finally got out of the huge rut I was stuck in.

The same is true in life. At times, we can get stuck in ruts that we simply can't get out of without the help of others. Some of us try harder when we get in a rut, and that often makes the rut deeper and even harder to get out of.

There are some ruts in life where you need friends, a wise counselor, or a professional to help you get free. Although God is all-powerful, He often chooses to work through others to help you become all that you were created to be.

I am very thankful for the wise men and women God has placed in my life to help me get out of the mental, emotional, and spiritual ruts that life inevitably brings.

I will never forget the wisdom, counsel, and prayer support of a minister named Stelman Smith and a family friend named Maureen Donohue. Both have since gone on to eternity, and I miss them dearly. I thank God for their blessing and influence in my life, as they helped me process different challenges and battles.

I have heard it said, "We are only as healthy as the secrets we don't keep." I try to live with no secrets. I processed many of mine with Stelman and Maureen, and today I am blessed with wise and godly counselors and advisors, including Paul MacMillan, Jay McCumber, and Nancy (Crickett) Barazotto. I can call them anytime, 24/7, to process and pray about any fear, doubt, or challenge.

The Scriptures tell us to "...confess your sins to one another, and pray for one another so that you may be healed..."[17] We all need friends we can confess our sins to.

At the time of this writing, I meet with a group of guys each Wednesday morning from 7 a.m. to 8:15 a.m. for breakfast. Together, we share life's joys and challenges, and many of us feel comfortable calling each other to confess a sin or request a specific prayer.

When you acknowledge and confess your sins, doubts, fears, and failures, God brings healing to help you out of the ruts that tend to trap and hold you back from becoming all He created and desires you to be.

I love the Proverb that reminds us, "As iron sharpens iron, so one person sharpens another."[18] We need others to sharpen us, just as we are called to sharpen others.

COMMUNITY OF MARRIAGE

Gayle and I met after our freshman year in college. Our first date was a Baltimore Orioles baseball game at old Memorial Stadium. I can still remember exactly what she wore—a blue jean skirt and a blue-and-white striped sleeveless shirt. She looked beautiful!

It took a number of years, but as I began to grow in my relationship with God while I was at Cornell, and Gayle began to grow in her relationship with God while she was at Mary Washington University, we started to grow closer and closer together.

We got married on August 22, 1987, at St. Joseph Catholic Church in Cockeysville, Maryland. Our main scripture from the wedding was from Ecclesiastes, a book in the Old Testament: "Two are better than one, because they have a good return for their labor: If either of them falls down, one can help the other up. But pity anyone who falls and has no one to help them up. Also, if two lie down together, they will keep warm. But how can one keep warm alone? Though one may be overpowered, two can defend themselves. A cord of three strands is not quickly broken."[19]

We knew we wanted God to be the third strand of our marriage cord. We believed that by inviting Jesus into our marriage, which we did, our three-strand cord would "not be quickly torn." By God's grace, as of this writing, we are approaching forty years of marriage.

Another scripture read at our wedding came from the Apostle Paul's letter to the church in Ephesus, and said, "Submit to one another out of reverence for Christ. Wives, submit yourselves to your own husbands as you do to the Lord. For the husband is the head of the wife as Christ is the head of the church . . . Husbands, love your wives, just as Christ loved the church and gave Himself up for her..."[20]

We were being called to submit to one another, to respect one another, and to love one another. And although Gayle was being called to submit to my leadership as the spiritual head of the family, I was called to give up, or be willing to sacrifice, my entire life for Gayle, as Jesus sacrificed His life for the church.

Another common reading at weddings comes from the Gospel of Matthew and says, "'For this reason a man will leave his father and mother and be united to his wife, and the two will become one flesh.' So they are no longer two, but one flesh. Therefore what God has joined together, let no one separate."[21]

This marriage thing is serious business—to become a cord of three strands, to be willing to die for my wife, and to remember that our marriage commitment and sacrament mean we are no longer two but one flesh. Talk about a supernatural, new community.

A GROWING FAMILY COMMUNITY

When Gayle and I got married, we knew we would face fertility challenges. Miraculously, God chose to bless us with two children through natural birth (Frankie and Stephen) and two through adoption (Jackie and JK). Our personal family community was growing.

The Scriptures remind us, "Children are a heritage from the Lord, offspring a reward from Him. Like arrows in the hands of a warrior are children born in one's youth. Blessed is the man whose quiver is full of them."[22]

As our children grew, Gayle and I were encouraged by God's Word from the book of Deuteronomy: "Hear, O Israel: The Lord our God, the Lord is one. Love the Lord your God with all your heart and with all your soul and with all your strength. These commandments that I give you today are to be on your hearts. Impress them on your children. Talk about them when you sit at home and when you walk along the road, when you lie down and when you get up."[23]

The commandments God gave us were to be on our hearts, and we were to impress them on our children. We were called to talk about God's commandments when we sat at home, when we walked (or drove) along the road, when we lay down (at night), and when we got up (in the morning).

We desired to share God's love and truth with our children in a way that each of their relationships with Him might become personal, real, and life-changing. As parents, we're challenged in God's Word, "do not exasperate your children; instead, bring them up in the training and instruction of the Lord,"[24] and to "train up our children in the way they should go, and even when they are old, they will not depart from it."[25] We didn't want to harass or overwhelm our children, but instead guide them to seek God's love and truth for themselves.

Gayle and I understand that our children need to make their own decisions about their faith and relationships with God. Yet, God's Word challenges children to "Listen . . . to your father's instruction and do not forsake your mother's teaching. They are a garland to grace your head and a chain to adorn your neck."[26] Family relationships that honor God involve listening, learning, and respect.

In most cases, we only have our children in our homes and under our direction until they are somewhere between the ages of eighteen and twenty-four, when they leave and embark on their adult lives. At that time, we are still family and a unique and special community, but it will never be the same as it once was. We are called to release our children as arrows launched into the world, with the hope that they will honor God and build new relationships and communities of their own.

Gayle and I are now empty nesters. Each of our children and two daughters-in-law are in a different place in their faith journeys. Some in our family are still questioning and deciding if they want to go "all in" and follow Jesus. Others are living out their faith and relationships with God in beautiful and tangible ways. It is true that parenting never ends, and we are thankful and love our children and grandchildren and cherish the time we get to spend together as a family.

PLEASE, SORRY, THANKS

Gayle and I now have more time to invest in other relationships, community activities, and organizations. For several years, we have hosted a church small group in our home on Tuesday nights. Gayle also finds community and fellowship through her involvement with Community Bible Study (CBS) and serves on several nonprofit boards. I also have a number of other boards and groups of which I am a member. No matter the group, it's always about people and relationships.

My mom raised my brothers and me to have empathetic hearts. Growing up, her sister Joan had special needs, so my mom always challenged us to care for every classmate or teammate, and especially those who might be left out or overlooked by others.

She encouraged us to be a "there you are" person instead of a "here I am" person. You know the difference. "There you are" people ask questions about you, your family, and your life. "Here I am" people let conversations revolve around themselves, and by the end of a party, social function, or round of golf, they know nothing about you.

I aspire to be an empathetic "there you are" person who helps build true community. I agree with the statement, "Empathy is the crown jewel of emotional intelligence."

Since relationships and community are keys to success in life, I have come to appreciate a practical reminder that a great way to bless and strengthen any relationship—even our relationship with God—is by using three simple words: Please, Sorry, and Thanks. Bestselling author Mark Batterson even wrote a book titled *Please, Sorry, Thanks: The Three Words That Change Everything.*

In his book, Batterson suggests that the greatest predictor of success in life and in our relationships—whether with family, friends, coworkers, teammates, and even our relationship with God—is our proficiency in using the words, Please, Sorry, and Thanks.[27] He notes that humbly using these words can shift the atmosphere at home, change the culture at work, and help you win friends and influence people. They will also help you and me bless and honor God.

I call these "respect" words. When we say "Please," offer "Sorry" when we make a mistake, and express "Thanks," we show respect and love.

As Batterson says, "Nothing opens doors like please; nothing mends fences like sorry; nothing builds bridges like thanks."

When you think about your life, do you have a tendency to want to Go alone or with others?

Since life is all about relationships and community, the challenge is to love and go in fellowship with God and others in order to fulfill your potential and be the best door opener, fence mender, and bridge builder that you can be.

SUGGESTED PRAYER

Dear God,
I realize nothing is more important than a right relationship with You,
my family, others, and even myself. I also believe that one of the keys to
growing in those relationships is fellowship and community. Please lead
me to a community or small group where I can love and be loved, serve
and be served, know and be known, celebrate and be celebrated, and
learn and grow while helping others learn and grow as well.
In Jesus' name. Amen.

CHAPTER 9

The Power of Relationships and Community

TRUTH #9:

**There is nothing more important in life than relationships
and the best way to grow in your relationship with God,
others, and even yourself, is in community.**

QUESTIONS FOR REFLECTION

1. What do you think about the quote, "If you want to go fast, go alone. If you want to go far, go together"?

2. On a scale of 1 to 10, how would you rate your relationship with God? Family? Friends? Co-workers? Yourself? What stood out to you most from this chapter about those relationships?

3. Do you have people in your life like the four friends who carried their paralyzed friend to meet Jesus? Are you that type of friend to others? Explain.

4. The Scriptures tell us to "...confess your sins to one another and pray for one another, that you may be healed..." Do you have any friends with whom you confess your sins and share your secrets? Who are they?

5. What do you appreciate the most about the definition of true community as "a group where you love and are loved, serve and are served, know and are known, celebrate and are celebrated?" Have you ever experienced a small group, team, or community like that?

6. Do you learn more in circles or rows? What is your most important takeaway from this chapter about relationships, fellowship, and community?

The Power Over Our Enemy

TRUTH #10:

We have an enemy who desires to rob, kill, and destroy us,
yet victory, freedom, and abundant life are available
to us through Jesus Christ.

"The thief comes only to steal and kill and destroy;
I came that they may have life and have it abundantly."[1]

Jesus

Growing up playing high school and college football and lacrosse, a common saying from coaches and teammates was, "Keep your head on a swivel!"

Because football and lacrosse are fast-paced games with a lot of movement and physical contact, coaches wanted us to be constantly aware of what was happening around us. The last thing they wanted was for one of their players to get crushed or knocked out of a game by a hit or a block they didn't see coming. By moving your head from side to side, you could see what was going on all around you and avoid a "backdoor cut" or a "blindside hit" that could hurt you and your team.

I believe we receive a similar warning in God's Word about an opponent we all have—an enemy who wants to knock us out of the game of life or, at the very least, injure us so we can never fulfill our potential.

In the Apostle Peter's first letter to the early church, he wrote, "Be alert [*keep your head on a swivel!*] and of sober mind. Your enemy the devil prowls around like a roaring lion looking for someone to devour."[2] Whether we realize it or not, we have an enemy who wants to rob, kill, and destroy us.

My friend and bestselling author Jon Gordon says, "Many think life is a playground, but it's really a battleground. It's scary to see so many people losing a battle they have no idea they are in. If you don't know you are in a battle, but your enemy does, you will surely lose. When you know you are in a battle and understand the enemy's game plan, you can prepare, counter it, and win it. And it's important to remember you can't win a spiritual battle with man-made strategies."[3]

A SPIRITUAL BATTLE

For the first twenty years of my life, I did not fully comprehend that we have an opponent or enemy who wants to destroy us. Many people today, even some who identify as Christians, don't believe in the devil or demons. This may even describe you, as it does a number of my friends.

As I began to read, study, and be exposed to God's Word and the wisdom of other more mature men and women of faith, I learned that we have an enemy—the devil, also known as Satan. He is often referred to in Scripture as "the father of lies,"[4] "the author of confusion,"[5] and "the thief [who] comes only to steal, kill, and destroy..."[6] And he has an army of fallen angels, known as demons or unclean spirits, who are an active part of his mission.

The Apostle Paul wrote in his letter to the Ephesians, "For our struggle is not against flesh and blood, but against the rulers, against the authorities, against the powers of this dark world and against the spiritual forces of evil in the heavenly realms."[7]

These statements and scriptures may raise questions in your heart and mind; they certainly did, and at times still do, in mine. If there is a spiritual battle, or invisible war, that rages, what do we need to know or be aware of to keep our spiritual head, heart, and mind on a swivel, and to avoid the plots, ploys, and plans of the enemy and his army?

We are wise to ask and consider:

- Who or what is this enemy referred to in Scripture as Satan, or the devil?

- Who are these authorities, powers of darkness, and spiritual forces of evil? How did they come to be, and do I actually believe that they exist?

- Does our enemy have a plan or strategy to hurt us and our families?

- Does God give us a strategy and plan to protect ourselves and our families?

- Is Jesus more powerful than our enemy?

C.S. Lewis, the famed British author and theologian, wrote a bestselling book about our enemy and spiritual warfare called *The Screwtape Letters*. In the preface, he notes, "There are two equal and opposite errors in which our race can fall about the devil(s). One is to disbelieve in his/their existence. The other is to believe, and to feel an excessive and unhealthy interest in them."[8]

In this book and in life, I seek to find the right balance.

Home Alone

I didn't realize it then, but the first time I experienced tangible spiritual warfare was when I was about twelve years old.

My parents had a meeting to attend, which they said would only take a couple of hours. They thought it would be fine to leave my three brothers and me at home, with me as the oldest in charge. Although they didn't tell us where they were going, it happened to be their first time attending a prayer meeting, which was being held in the basement of a local church.

Before leaving, my mom put some pizzas in the oven and told me to feed my brothers after the timer went off. When the oven buzzer sounded, I took out the pizzas, and my brothers and I ate most of them.

My next job was to make sure my youngest brothers, David and Bryan, got a bath. Once the bathtub was full, they got in and started playing around when they noticed a big spider on the ceiling. They decided to grab a roll of toilet paper, tear off pieces, get them wet, and try to hit the spider. By the time I got back into the bathroom, there were dozens of wet toilet paper balls stuck to the ceiling, with the spider still comfortably in place. I let my brother David, the older of the two, have it and told him he had better clean every piece of wet toilet paper off the ceiling.

David said he would take care of it—and boy, did he. He decided to get out of the tub, climb up on the sink, and stand on the towel rack to reach the wet toilet paper on the ceiling. As soon as he stepped on the towel rack, it tore completely off the wall, leaving two huge holes in the drywall.

We only had one family bathroom, so a few minutes later, my brother John came in to use the toilet. Unfortunately, when he flushed, the toilet overflowed all over the floor. It took a few minutes, but we found an apple core someone had flushed earlier, which caused the overflow.

We decided to wait a few minutes before cleaning up the bathroom and instead went into my parents' room to have a wrestling match on their bed.

It was my youngest brother Bryan and me against my brothers John and David. What started as a tag-team event quickly turned into a two-on-two brawl, with the first team to get both opponents off the bed declared winners.

Unfortunately, during the middle of our battle, one of the legs of my parents' bed collapsed. We scrambled to come up with a plan to fix it, and my brother David brought in two encyclopedias to hold up the bed. (I think it was "L" and "M," back when encyclopedias were alphabetized hardback books.)

Their bed wasn't perfectly even, but it was close enough. For some reason, we decided to go to bed after that. My parents had told me to make sure everyone was asleep by 9 p.m., so I wanted to make sure we were in bed before they got home.

What we didn't know was that night at the prayer meeting, which happened to be part of the Charismatic Renewal movement in the Catholic Church, my parents decided to fully surrender their lives to Jesus and ask the Holy Spirit to baptize and fill them. They came home as new creations in Christ, filled with the joy of the Lord.

We heard them come through the door but decided to pretend we were asleep.

As they tell the story, they were so excited about their new relationship with Jesus and the power and presence of the Holy Spirit. They had never experienced anything like it and were determined to live the rest of their lives dedicated to the Lord and filled with the love, joy, and peace of the Spirit.

Unfortunately, when they walked into the kitchen, they found leftover, half-eaten pizza on the counter and the oven still on, with small pieces of pizza inside that were black and smoking.

Then, my dad noticed a brown watery substance leaking through the family room ceiling onto the couch below. He ran upstairs and found about two inches of brown toilet water on the bathroom floor, the towel rack ripped out of the wall, and toilet paper stuck all over the ceiling.

He started yelling my name and my brothers' names. Even though we were pretending to be asleep, he got us out of bed to clean up what we could.

Later, my parents made their way into their bedroom and noticed their bed was cockeyed and about four inches too low on one side. That's when they found the "L" and "M" encyclopedia books holding up one corner of the bed.

We didn't realize it at the time, but I have come to believe that spiritual warfare raged and broke loose in our house that night as my parents entered into this new, personal, life-changing relationship with Jesus and the Holy Spirit. We would later learn that the enemy hates when people come to know the truth and will do everything possible, once we know the truth, to discourage us from sharing the Good News of Jesus Christ and His love with others.

Since then, I have had more intense personal encounters and warfare with the enemy, who seeks to rob, kill, and destroy us. One of his main goals is to keep us from experiencing the joy, peace, and blessings of a personal relationship with God, as well as the many blessings and opportunities God wants to provide if we choose to follow and serve Him.

THE DEVIL AND DEMONS – REALLY?

As I referenced earlier, many doubt and wonder if there really is an enemy—a devil and demons—and, if so, where did he/they come from, and how do they function in this modern age?

God's Word tells us that Lucifer was a powerful angel created by God. The name Lucifer means "bearer of light" or "morning star," and this name refers to the angel's former splendor before he defied God, fell from grace, and was cast out of heaven with the angels who fell with him, now known as demons or unclean spirits.

In the last book of the Bible, Revelation, we read, "Then war broke out in heaven. Michael [the Archangel] and his angels fought against the dragon [Satan], and the dragon and his angels fought back. But, he [the dragon] was not strong enough, and they lost their place in heaven. The great dragon was hurled down—the ancient serpent called the devil, or Satan, who leads the world astray. He was hurled to the earth and his angels with him."[9]

Other scriptures reference that the dragon's tail "swept a third of the stars out of the sky and flung them to the earth."[10] His sin of pride and wanting to be God, rather than serve or worship Him, led him and a third of all the angels who aligned with him to be cast out of heaven to wreak havoc on earth. Even Jesus said, "I saw Satan fall like lightning from heaven."[11]

It is encouraging to know that two-thirds of the angels remained loyal to God and, to this day, are called "holy angels."[12]

An Invisible War

Since Satan and his angels/demons fell, there has been a battle or spiritual warfare on earth. According to *The Invisible War* by Chip Ingram, there are five key things we should know about spiritual warfare:

1. There is an invisible world.

2. We are all involved in an invisible war.

3. Our enemy or foe is formidable.

4. We must be aware of and respect our foe/enemy, but not fear him.

5. We do not fight for victory; we fight from victory.[13]

The great news is that Jesus defeated Satan, sin, and death when His blood was shed on the cross and He rose from the dead. The Scriptures remind us that "...greater is He who is in you than he who is in the world."[14]

Because of Jesus, we win! Yet, even Jesus would have his own encounters and battles with Satan.

Temptation

After being baptized by John the Baptist and having the Holy Spirit descend on Him like a dove, Jesus went into the Judean Desert to fast and pray for forty days and nights. We read in the Gospel of Matthew:

> Then Jesus was led by the Spirit into the wilderness to be tempted by the devil. After fasting forty days and forty nights, he was hungry. The tempter came to him and said, "If you are the Son of God, tell these stones to become bread."
>
> Jesus answered, "It is written: 'Man shall not live on bread alone, but on every word that comes from the mouth of God.'"
>
> Then the devil took him to the holy city and had him stand on the highest point of the temple. "If you are the Son of God," he said, "throw yourself down. For it is written:
>
> "'He will command his angels concerning you, and they will lift you up in their hands, so that you will not strike your foot against a stone.'"
>
> Jesus answered him, "It is also written: 'Do not put the Lord your God to the test.'"
>
> Again, the devil took him to a very high mountain and showed him all the kingdoms of the world and their splendor. "All this I will give you," he said, "if you will bow down and worship me."
>
> Jesus said to him, "Away from me, Satan! For it is written: 'Worship the Lord your God and serve him only.'"
>
> Then the devil left him, and angels came and attended him.[15]

In this story, Satan used God's own words as recorded in Scripture to tempt and trick Jesus. Of course, the devil, being a deceiver, used the Word and truth out of context. Fortunately, Jesus, filled with the Spirit and full of wisdom, was able to combat the temptations, deceptions, and lies of the enemy with truth. Jesus responded to each temptation by quoting Scripture accurately and in context back to the enemy, which totally thwarted him. We can use this same strategy when the enemy tries to tempt, deceive, and ultimately destroy us.

Satan often tempts us like he tempted Jesus. However, if we fall, Satan then condemns us. His strategy is to minimize the sin before we do it and then maximize the sin after we do it.

Rick Warren reminds us, "What is the devil's work? He messes with your mind. He fills it with worry, guilt, resentment, anger, fear, and confusion. He whispers in your ear that you're worthless, helpless, hopeless, and aimless. Satan uses these thoughts and emotions to try and keep you enslaved."[16]

As already noted, Satan is a liar. As Scripture tells us, "When he lies, he speaks his native language, for he is a liar and the father of lies."[17]

And in the Apostle Paul's second letter to the Corinthians, we read, "...Satan disguises himself as an angel of light. Therefore it is not surprising if his servants also disguise themselves as servants of righteousness..."[18]

We must be on guard for the deception and tricks of the enemy.

OUR BODY IS A HOUSE

We must remember that the angels who fell with Satan still roam the earth as demons or unclean spirits. In the Scriptures, our human body is often referenced as a "house" or "dwelling place." Jesus said, "Behold, I stand at the door and knock; if anyone hears My voice and opens the door, I will come in to him and will dine with him, and he with Me."[19]

If we open the door of our hearts and invite Jesus into our lives, He promises to come in and, along with the Holy Spirit, live in and through us. Likewise, we can open our lives to the enemy and demonic occupation and not even know it.

Jesus is gracious and will only come in if we open the door of our hearts and invite Him in. However, our enemy—spiritual forces of darkness—will try to enter our lives in any way possible. Deception and trickery are methods the enemy and his minions use every day to get people to open their lives, whether knowingly or unknowingly, and when they come, they bring evil and darkness with them.

We can inadvertently let the enemy into our lives by not understanding the dangers of the occult, which means "the secret or hidden realm," often as it relates to the devil and his demons. Many people think this is a joke, but God's Word makes it clear that we should avoid things like witchcraft, fortune-telling, palm reading, communication with the dead, sorcery, Ouija boards, Satanism, and channeling, to name a few.

If you have had any contact with the occult or demonic activity—even if it was a long time ago and just for fun—it would be wise to verbally renounce your involvement, ask for God's forgiveness, and seek deliverance ministry if needed. In extreme cases, there are trained ministers and clergy who, through specific prayer, call upon the power of Jesus and the Holy Spirit to dispel any demonic entity or entities believed to be harassing, oppressing, or possessing the body of a person.

One of the best books I have read about spiritual warfare and overcoming demonic strongholds, negative thoughts, irrational feelings, and habitual sins is *The Bondage Breaker* by Neil Anderson. In it, he reminds us, "It isn't power that sets the captives free, it is truth."[20]

He points to the Gospel of John, where Jesus reminds His followers, "If you hold to my teaching, you are really my disciples. Then you will know the truth, and the truth will set you free."[21] Later in the Gospel of John, Jesus said, "I am the way and the truth and the life..."[22]

Anderson notes, "The power of Satan is in the lie. The power of the Christian (or followers of Jesus) is in the truth."

Jesus Christ is the truth, the bondage breaker, and the only one who can give us true victory and freedom.

Victory and Freedom

In the Gospels, we read multiple stories of Jesus setting people free from demonic strongholds, bondage, and even possession—men, women, and even children.

There was the mute, demon-possessed man who was brought to Jesus in the town of Capernaum, on the north shore of the Sea of Galilee, where Jesus was living. In the Gospel of Matthew, we read, "After the demon was cast out, the mute man spoke; and the crowds were amazed, and were saying, 'Nothing like this has ever been seen in Israel.'"[23]

Then, there was another man who lived on the other side of the Sea of Galilee in the country of the Gerasenes who was also demon-possessed. The Gospel of Mark notes, "When He [Jesus] got out of the boat, immediately a man from the tombs with an unclean spirit met Him . . . and no one was able to bind him anymore, not even with a chain..."[24]

Jesus ultimately set the man free from "a legion" of demons. When Jesus got back into His boat to return to Capernaum, "the man who had been demon-possessed begged to go with him. Jesus did not let him, but said, 'Go home to your own people and tell them how much the Lord has done for you, and how he has had mercy on you.'"[25]

We also see in the Gospel of Luke a reference to "...some women who had been healed of evil spirits and sicknesses: Mary who was called Magdalene, from whom seven demons had gone out..."[26]

Mary Magdalene, who was set free by Jesus, became one of His closest followers and a witness to His crucifixion and resurrection. She is remembered and celebrated to this day for her life transformation and the way she blessed and served Jesus.

Each of these stories reminds us that Jesus is greater than our enemy and has the power to set free anyone who turns to Him.

The Five D's

While people today are still susceptible to demonic oppression, harassment, attachment, or, in extreme cases, possession by evil and unclean spirits, a more common experience of spiritual warfare is subtle.

I appreciate how Jon Gordon explains in his book *The Garden* the strategies and tactics the enemy uses every day to try to defeat and destroy us. Gordon refers to the enemy's efforts as The Five D's: *Doubt, Distortion, Discouragement, Distraction,* and *Division.*

The enemy wants to create doubt that God and His Word can't be trusted. Gordon reminds us that the enemy wants us to believe there is no God and, therefore, no miracles. The enemy is skilled at making people doubt and ignore God and His miracles that exist all around them.

The enemy wants to distort the truth with lies. As we know, the enemy is a liar, and he wants to fill our minds with falsehoods.

The enemy ultimately distorts truth with lies to cause doubt, in order to discourage us. Gordon reminds us that we are not the source of our own negative thoughts. Instead of listening to the lies, we need to talk to ourselves with truth. As Jesus did to Satan, we must speak truth to the lies and remember that what God says about us is the ultimate truth.

The enemy wants to distract us from the things in life that matter most—our relationship with God, our relationship with family and others, and becoming all that God created us to be.

And the enemy's ultimate goal is to divide and separate us from God. He seeks to divide us in order to defeat us.

The enemy distracts, discourages, distorts, and creates doubt so we will be divided from God, divided from each other, and even divided from our true selves and thus not fulfilling our God-given potential.

The good news is that God has a clear plan for us to overcome and defeat the plots, ploys, and plans of the enemy.

THE ARMOR OF GOD

In various sports, players wear equipment like helmets to protect their heads, and they wear shoulder pads, elbow pads, gloves, and more to protect their bodies. Fortunately, God provides us with spiritual equipment to protect us from the attacks of the enemy and his army.

God challenges us to be strong in the Lord and His mighty power. Through the Apostle Paul, the Holy Spirit wrote:

> Therefore put on the full armor [or equipment] of God, so that when the day of evil comes, you may be able to stand your ground... Stand firm then, with the belt of truth buckled around your waist, with the breastplate of righteousness in place, and with your feet fitted with the readiness that comes from the gospel of peace. In addition to all this, take up the shield of faith, with which you can extinguish all the flaming arrows of the evil one. Take the helmet of salvation and the sword of the Spirit, which is the word of God.[27]

Like a good coach who wants their players to be properly equipped and protected, God gives us the spiritual equipment to "put on" to win the invisible war we continually face. Our own strength is never sufficient to oppose Satan and his army, but God provides us access to His strength and equipment to win.

When Paul wrote this letter to the church in Ephesus, most of the world was under Roman rule. Paul used analogies or word pictures that would make sense at that time. He identified six pieces of armor that God provides to help us withstand any attack from our spiritual enemy.

The Belt of Truth

The belt was essential for a Roman soldier, holding his armor together and keeping his weapons within reach. Similarly, we need to know and have easy access to the truth, God's Word, to combat the schemes of the enemy. We know Satan and his army are masters of lies and deception, but by knowing, applying, and speaking God's Word and truth, we can overcome the lies and the liar.

The Breastplate of Righteousness

No Roman soldier would go into battle without his breastplate, which protected his torso and vital organs. We are made righteous by God's grace through faith in Jesus Christ, and must remember that the mind and the emotions are two areas where the enemy most fiercely attacks believers. He desires to snatch the Word of God from our minds and replace it with his own perverse ideas. Our protection against Satan's attacks is the breastplate of righteousness, as God's righteousness protects us from spiritual assaults, just as the Roman soldier's breastplate protected him from physical assaults.

The Shoes of the Gospel of Peace

A soldier whose feet were blistered, cut, or swollen could not fight well, putting him in serious danger. Our spiritual footwear is equally important in our warfare against the schemes of the devil. Through Jesus, we have constant access to "the peace of God, which transcends all understanding, will guard your hearts and your minds..."[28] If we are in Christ, our feet are firmly rooted on the solid ground of the gospel of peace, and the truth that God is our Father, our friend, and our defender.

The Shield of Faith

Roman soldiers carried large wooden shields, covered with metal or thick leather, to guard their whole bodies. Enemies fired flaming arrows—with tips wrapped in pitch-soaked cloths, lit before release. On impact, the burning pitch splattered, igniting anything flammable. We need a shield of faith to "distinguish all the flaming arrows of the evil one."

Our enemy continually bombards us with flaming arrows of fear, despair, pride, lust, anger, hatred, covetousness, and other temptations. Ultimately, every flaming arrow or temptation tries to get us to doubt or distrust God and drive a wedge between us. We need to use our faith as a shield to make sure that doesn't happen.

The Helmet of Salvation

The helmet protects the head, a vital area in battle. Paul references the helmet of salvation as a reminder that the enemy wants to undermine our faith, hope, security, and assurance of salvation in Christ, with the goal of creating discouragement and doubt. The enemy wants us to lose confidence in the love and care of our heavenly Father. The helmet of salvation reminds us of God's goodness, care, and promise to never leave or forsake us.

The Sword of the Spirit

The final piece of armor Paul mentions is "the sword of the Spirit, which is the word of God." It is a key weapon of defense against the onslaught of Satan and his army. When Jesus was tempted by Satan in the wilderness, His defense for each of Satan's temptations was proclaiming scripture that precisely contradicted it. The Holy Spirit can empower us to use God's Word and truth to combat and thwart our enemy.

The Blood of Jesus

The most costly and significant weapon Jesus makes available to us is His shed blood on the cross.

Andre Ngambu, in his book *The Blood of Jesus Christ in Spiritual Warfare*, writes, "In spiritual warfare, the blood of Jesus is a very powerful weapon that gives us victory over Satan and all his acolytes [followers]. It is both an offensive and defensive weapon. With His blood, Jesus purchased our authority and deliverance. The blood breaks addictions, breaks spiritual bondages, and subdues the work of the enemy. In Christ, we have authority before Satan and his army, when we declare the truth that 'Satan is defeated by the blood of Jesus Christ' and to this, all his accusations lose power."[29]

The Word of God declares in the book of Revelation how to overcome and defeat the father of lies and our accuser, saying, "And they overcame him by the blood of the Lamb, and by the word of their testimony...."[30]

About a thousand years before the time of Jesus, God told Moses that the Israelites should put the blood of a Passover lamb on their doorposts as a sign to the angel of death to pass over their homes during what would be the final plague on Pharaoh and the Egyptian people.[31]

God's chosen people, the Israelites, were spared by the blood of the lamb, just as those of us who call on Jesus and depend on His shed blood on the cross are spared today. Through His blood, the Father passes over our sins and welcomes us into a personal relationship with Him, and through His blood, we render the enemy powerless.

For those who celebrate Communion at church, we are reminded of and experience both the body and blood of Jesus—"...the Lamb of God, who takes away the sin of the world!"[32] That same blood has the power to thwart Satan and his army of demons.

HE'S ON A LEASH!

When I think about our enemy and spiritual warfare, I am reminded of a story about my friend Dan Britton. Dan was a major leader in the growth of FCA around the world, visiting more than sixty different countries on behalf of the ministry.

Everywhere Dan goes, he makes it a priority to start his morning with a five-mile run, even when he doesn't know exactly where he is going. One morning in South Korea, Dan was halfway through his daily run when he suddenly heard and saw a huge dog coming after him. His adrenaline escalated, and his heart rate accelerated as he picked up the pace, sprinting to escape the dog's imminent attack.

The dog was only a few feet away from pouncing on Dan when it was suddenly yanked back; it was on a long leash that ran out. As Dan's adrenaline and heart rate settled back to a normal rate, he breathed a huge sigh of relief.

The next morning, Dan ran the same route. That same dog came at him again, running around barking. But this time, Dan knew the dog was on a leash. He was certainly not going to enter the dog's space, where he could get mauled or even killed, but he had nothing to fear as long as he kept his distance.

In many ways, this story is a great illustration of our enemy, the devil. He prowls around like a lion, seeking someone to devour. But ultimately, our enemy is on a leash. If we don't step into the enemy's space, he can't harm us. However, we need to be aware and keep our spiritual head on a swivel.

We are wise to heed the words written by James, "Submit therefore to God. Resist the devil and he will flee from you."[33]

THE ENEMY'S ULTIMATE GOAL

The No. 1 goal of the enemy is to keep you and me from choosing to believe, receive, and follow Jesus. He does not want us to experience the abundant or eternal life Jesus desires for us, nor does he want us to walk and live in the purpose and power God has prepared for us.

If our enemy fails in his first mission and we do come to know and embrace the truth, his second goal is to keep us from helping anyone else in our sphere of influence from coming to believe, receive, and follow Jesus. As the father of lies, he will do everything possible to keep us from the truth about Jesus and the beauty and power of a personal relationship with Him.

The good news is that we win. We have victory over our enemy and can help others experience victory and freedom if we are willing to listen, learn, and apply God's Word and truth to our lives.

Although Satan is very powerful and carries on a worldwide mission of evil and deception, he is a created being. Unlike God, Satan is not omnipresent, omniscient, or omnipotent. He and his army of demons cannot read your mind, and they do not know the future. But the devil is an expert on human behavior and weakness, and he looks for opportunities to enter, harass, and oppress us. When we are attacked, if we speak truth out loud to the enemy, as Jesus did, our enemy will ultimately flee.

Are you ready to *Go* to battle? Are you prepared to help yourself, your family, and your friends have victory over our enemy and experience the freedom and abundant life Jesus offers?

The enemy's strategy is clear, yet with God's Word and game plan, we can *love* and *go* and say with confidence, "...Thanks be to God, who gives us the victory through our Lord Jesus Christ."[34]

SUGGESTED PRAYER

Dear God,

Please protect my family and me from the plots, ploys, and plans of our enemy—the devil and his demons. Thank You, Jesus, for dying on the cross, shedding Your blood to cleanse and cover my sin, and rising from the dead to defeat Satan and his army. Please help me to love and go in your truth, victory, freedom, and abundant life.

In Jesus' name. Amen.

The Power Over Our Enemy

TRUTH #10:

**We have an enemy who desires to rob, kill, and destroy us,
yet victory, freedom, and abundant life are available
to us through Jesus Christ.**

QUESTIONS FOR REFLECTION

1. What did you learn about our enemy and spiritual warfare from this chapter? Do you believe in Satan (the devil) and/or demons and unclean spirits? Why or why not?

2. How did the devil treat Jesus after He had fasted for forty days and forty nights? What did Jesus do to crush the enemy's temptation efforts?

3. Have you had any experiences with spiritual warfare that you are aware of and are willing to share? How does the enemy tend to tempt or attack you?

4. What goes through your mind when you think about The Five D's of *Doubt, Distortion, Discouragement, Distraction,* and *Division* that Jon Gordon shares in his book *The Garden*?

5. What strikes you about the story of my friend Dan and the dog on a leash? Have you done anything to expose your life to attack from the enemy?

6. Which piece(s) of The Armor of God in Ephesians 6 are most practical to you? Why?

CHAPTER 11

The Power of Creation

TRUTH #11:

**God created the universe, and He created each of us
in His image, to be creators as well.**

"In the beginning God created the heavens and the earth."[1]

Moses

I'll never forget the call I received on the evening of March 11, 2020. I was at home putting the finishing touches on my presentation for our annual corporate meeting the next morning. It was our Senior Vice President of Marketing and Communications, Jen Silberzahn, calling to discuss whether we should cancel the meeting in light of the news about the rapidly spreading COVID-19 virus.

Businesses, schools, and even churches were being strongly advised to cease operations and encourage their people to work, study, and even worship from home.

How would our business survive? After nearly forty-five years in operation, how could we continue to serve and retain our clients when only a handful of our nearly 500 associates, deemed "essential employees" by the government, would be allowed on-site at our corporate headquarters?

With less than twelve hours' notice, we made the difficult decision to cancel our corporate meeting that our team had worked so hard to prepare for. Instead, the next day, we began the process of implementing a remote work plan. Within days, the COVID-19 pandemic shut down most of the world.

Somehow, our amazing leadership and technology teams figured out how to equip our people to serve our clients remotely from their homes. There was still a lot of work to be done, but the pace of life slowed down significantly. Sports and other activities were canceled, and travel was severely restricted.

I was driving my wife Gayle crazy working from home, so to get out of the house, I began taking lots of walks—very long walks.

At first, I spent most of my walks on the phone, checking in with family and friends and dealing with various business challenges and issues. But over time, I started doing something I had never done before. Whenever I came across a bird or flower of note, I would use my iPhone to take a picture of it.

Later, as I looked closely and zoomed in on those pictures, I marveled at the incredible detail and beauty of the birds and flowers I had previously taken for granted. Looking at those pictures, I would often ask myself, *"How did God do that?"* and *"Why did God do that?"* Creation was speaking to me in a way I had never before seen, heard, or fully considered.

A scripture that encouraged me as I reflected on these pictures comes from the Gospel of Matthew where Jesus said, "Look at the birds of the air; they do not sow or reap or store away in barns, and yet your heavenly Father feeds them..."[2] And then, "See how the flowers of the field grow. They do not labor or spin. Yet I tell you that not even Solomon [the richest person to ever live] in all his splendor was dressed like one of these . . . So do not worry..."[3]

The following year, with encouragement from some family and friends, I compiled my favorite "Look at the birds of the air" and "See the flowers of the field" pictures, along with my thoughts and reflections, into a colorful coffee table book titled *Look & See*.

I have always loved and admired creation, but putting that book together challenged me to consider its depth, power, and beauty in a whole new way.

CREATION STORIES

Did you know that over the millennia, more than one hundred different creation stories or myths have been recorded? Since the beginning of mankind, people have asked, "How did the world and all of life come into existence? Did God or a higher power create it, or was it random chance?"

Some believe there is no God or Creator and that billions of years ago, a dense fireball appeared out of nowhere and exploded, setting the universe into motion. They believe the universe and all of life have evolved ever since. But for me, there is too much order in the world, and life is too amazing to believe the universe and all of life came from nothing without an eternal, all-powerful Creator.

The very first verse in the Bible makes it clear: "In the beginning God created the heavens and the earth."[4] As we read further, we see that He created all of life, including each of us, in His image, to be co-creators as well.

Maybe God used a huge explosion to begin the process, but believing in a Big Bang without a Creator or master plan is like believing a huge explosion in a print shop could produce a perfect A-to-Z dictionary.

The first book of the Bible, Genesis, actually contains two complementary creation accounts accepted in today's Jewish, Christian, and Islamic faiths.

The phrase "God said" appears ten times in the first chapter of Genesis to describe the creation of the world and all that dwells in it. The Psalms affirm this truth: "For he spoke, and it came to be; he commanded, and it stood firm."[5]

We are told God spoke the world into existence over a period of six days and rested on the seventh. Whether these were literal twenty-four-hour days or God's "...a day is like a thousand years, and a thousand years are like a day,"[6] only He knows.

Exactly *how* He spoke creation into existence, we are not sure. *Why* He did it, other than to bless us, only He knows for certain. *Who* did it? All the evidence points to an all-powerful, all-knowing, everywhere-present Creator and triune God.

Let's take a closer look at God's creation story in Genesis to better understand how and what He created each day and what part we may have in creation stories going forward.

Day 1: Light and Darkness

In the beginning God created the heavens and the earth. Now the earth was formless and empty, darkness was over the surface of the deep, and the Spirit of God was hovering over the waters.

And God said, "Let there be light," and there was light. God saw that the light was good, and he separated the light from the darkness. God called the light "day" and the darkness he called "night." And there was evening, and there was morning—the first day.[7]

God created light, which is central to life, and Jesus is called the "Light of the World."[8] Without light, life as we know it could not exist. Every form of life relies on light, whether directly or indirectly. Plants use light to generate energy through photosynthesis, which sustains the entire food chain. The intricate balance between light and life reveals the brilliance of God's design.

Day 2: Sky and Waters

And God said, "let there be a vault between the waters to separate water from water." So God made the vault and separated the water under the vault from the water above it. And it was so. God called the vault "sky." And there was evening, and there was morning—the second day.[9]

Why did God make the sky blue during the day and dark at night? Despite what two of my brothers and two sons who graduated from the University of North Carolina think, it's not because God is a Tar Heel and loves Carolina Blue.

Sunlight reaches the Earth's atmosphere and is scattered in all directions by the gases and particles in the air. Blue light is scattered more than other colors because it travels as shorter, smaller waves. This is why we see a blue sky most of the time.[10]

Many say the fact that the Earth is ideally suited for human life is evidence of a wise Creator. Earth's atmosphere is perfectly tuned to sustain life. The sky shields us from UV radiation, stabilizes temperatures, and the precise mixture of oxygen, nitrogen, and trace gases allows us to breathe.

The water cycle continuously refreshes Earth's surface, involving evaporation, condensation, and precipitation. Scientists have yet to find another planet with a system so perfectly designed to support life.

How did God do that?

Day 3: Land, Seas, and Vegetation

And God said, "Let the water under the sky be gathered to one place, and let dry ground appear." And it was so. God called the dry ground "land," and the gathered waters he called "seas." And God saw that it was good.

Then God said, "Let the land produce vegetation: seed-bearing plants and trees on the land that bear fruit with seed in it, according to their various kinds." And it was so. The land produced vegetation: plants bearing seed according to their kinds and trees bearing fruit with seed in it according to their kinds. And God saw that it was good. And there was evening, and there was morning—the third day.[11]

With over 400,000 plant species and 2,000 types of fruit, including 7,500 varieties of apples, God did not skimp. Trees alone exceed 73,000 species, playing vital roles in air purification, climate regulation, and soil preservation.

Consider how every fruit and seed is designed to regenerate, provide nourishment, and sustain ecosystems. What is amazing about any seed is that if you plant it, it will grow and bear much more fruit, which will contain even more seeds with the potential for new life.

Most of the Earth's water is contained in its global ocean, covering nearly 71 percent of its crust or surface. The ocean is home to over 2 million species, and for some reason, God created the ocean water to have the exact salt levels required to sustain all of that life.

How and why did God do that?

Day 4: Sun, Moon, and Stars

And God said, "Let there be lights in the vault of the sky to separate the day from the night, and let them serve as signs to mark sacred times, and days and years, and let them be lights in the vault of the sky to give light on the earth." And it was so. God made two great lights—the greater light to govern the day and the lesser light to govern the night. He also made the stars. God set them in the vault of the sky to give light on the earth, to govern the day and the night, and to separate light from darkness. And God saw that it was good. And there was evening, and there was morning—the fourth day.[12]

God placed the sun to govern the day and the moon to govern the night. The sun, 110 times Earth's size, fuels life through photosynthesis. The moon's gravitational pull creates tides, stabilizing Earth's rotation and creating boundaries for the oceans that have existed for thousands of years. You can even measure the tides—high, low, and in between, to the exact minute, every day of every year.

The sun—a nearly perfect sphere of hot plasma radiating energy—orbits the Galactic Center of the Milky Way, about 25,000 light-years away.[13] A light-year is the distance light travels in one Earth year—about 6 trillion miles (picture the number six with twelve zeros after it).

At the same time, the Earth rotates around its axis in slightly less than a day (twenty-three hours and fifty-six minutes). The axis is tilted, which produces the four seasons. And although the moon produces no light of its own, it is lit by sun rays reflecting off its surface.

God creates in many ways!

The Eagle Has Landed

Talking about the moon, I will never forget July 21, 1969, when I was just five years old. My younger brother John and I were in Ocean City, New Jersey, swimming in a motel pool with my father when my mom called us to come back into the room.

It was around 10 p.m., which was late for me and John, but my parents wanted us to witness the miraculous and historic effort of three American astronauts landing the Apollo II lunar module, Eagle, on the moon's surface.

Traveling 238,900 miles from Cape Kennedy (now known as Cape Canaveral) to the Sea of Tranquility—not a water sea, but a smooth surface area on the moon—was a highly risky and dangerous mission. After the Apollo II lunar module successfully touched down, astronaut Neil Armstrong famously announced, "The Eagle has landed."

Shortly after, Armstrong descended the nine-rung ladder of the Eagle, holding onto its side rails. When his oversized left moon boot made its impression on the desolate surface, the moon dust was as fine as talcum. "Like powdered charcoal," Armstrong would later describe the footprint left by the footstep that became the most-watched event in human history.

Armstrong then uttered the words that will never be forgotten, "That's one small step for man, one giant leap for mankind."[14]

God allowed mankind to create a rocket and lunar module, to circle the moon, land on its surface, and return safely to Earth. What a powerful and historic way to experience God's creation.

Shining Stars

Not only does the moon reflect the sun's light, but it shares the expanse with too many stars to count. Yet, these stars are not scattered randomly through space; they are gathered into vast groups called galaxies. The sun, an ordinary star in the Milky Way Galaxy, regulates Earth's weather, ocean currents, seasons, and climate. It makes plant life possible through photosynthesis. Without the sun's heat and light, life on Earth would not exist.

Astronomers estimate there are more than 100 billion stars in the Milky Way Galaxy alone. And most place the total number of galaxies to be at least 200 billion.

Are you kidding me? Two hundred billion galaxies, each with hundreds of millions of stars?

I can totally relate to King David, who wrote, "When I consider your heavens, the work [creation] of your fingers, the moon and the stars, which you have set in place, what is mankind that you are mindful of them, human beings that you care for them."[15]

The Psalmist also wrote about God: "He determines the number of the stars and calls them each by name."[16]

How and why did God create so many planets, moons, and stars and call them each by name?

Day 5: Sea Creatures and Birds

And God said, "Let the water teem with living creatures, and let birds fly above the earth across the vault of the sky." So God created the great creatures of the sea and every living thing with which the water teems and that moves about it in it, according to their kinds, and every winged bird according to its kind. And God saw that it was good. God blessed them and said, "Be fruitful and increase in number and fill the water in the seas, and let the birds increase on the earth." And there was evening, and there was morning—the fifth day.[17]

When God created the great creatures of the sea and every living and moving thing with which the water teems, He did not cut any corners.

God chose to create more than 2 million species of creatures, each according to its kind, to live in the ocean. Marine species range in size from microscopic phytoplankton, as small as 0.02 micrometers, to the blue whale, Earth's largest animal, which can grow over 100 feet long and weigh up to 200 tons.

Incredibly, there are more than 35,000 species of fish, and scientists estimate there are about 3.5 trillion fish swimming on Earth today. Wow!

And for those who love watching "Shark Week," it's estimated there are more than 400 different kinds of sharks, totaling over 1 billion sharks in all the oceans around the world.

How and why did God do all of that?

This is the same question I ask when I play on the beach with our grandchildren and dig up dozens of sand crabs that live five to six inches below the wet ocean sand. The only thing I think they are good for is surf fishing bait, but I'm sure God created them for more reasons than that.

Fish and sea animals reproduce in various ways depending on the species, but most produce sexually, an example of how God allows male and female fish to participate in the creation process.

I have no idea *how* or *why* God chose to create fish and other sea creatures in these ways, but it keeps on working and has since the beginning of creation. Thank You, Lord!

Birds, numbering over 11,000 species, display stunning colors from vibrant red and blue to subtle brown, gray, and black. Many colors help birds blend in and stay camouflaged from predators, while brighter colors can show off a bird's strength and health or warn predators.

God created birds to share in His creation process as well. The male passes sperm inside the female to fertilize her eggs, which, in most species, are nested and incubated by her until birth. Miraculous!

The flight of birds remains one of nature's most fascinating feats. Their wings, feathers, and lightweight bones are masterfully designed for efficiency. Some birds migrate thousands of miles, navigated by Earth's magnetic field. How did they learn this?

Every detail points to intentional design by an all-powerful Creator.

Day 6: Land Animals and Humans

And God said, "Let the land produce living creatures according to their kinds: the livestock, the creatures that move along the ground, and the wild animals, each according to its kind." And it was so. God made the wild animals according to their kinds, the livestock according to their kinds, and all the creatures that move along the ground according to their kinds. And God saw that it was good.

Then God said, "Let us make mankind in our image, in our likeness, so that they may rule over the fish in the sea and the birds in the sky, over the livestock and all the wild animals, and over all the creatures that move along the ground . . .

So . . . God created mankind in his own image, in the image of God he created them; male and female he created them.

God blessed them and said to them, "Be fruitful and increase in number; fill the earth and subdue it. Rule over the fish in the sea and the birds in the sky and over every living creature that moves on the ground . . .

...God saw all that he had made, and it was very good. And there was evening, and there was morning—the sixth day.[18]

Over 1.5 million animal species live on Earth's land surface, and over 1 million of those are insects. The smallest insect is the tiny wasp known as a fairyfly, whose males are wingless and measure only 0.005 inches long. The largest land animal is the African elephant, which can stand up to thirteen feet tall, stretch sixteen feet long, and weigh nearly seven tons.

God made more than 10,000 species of reptiles, ranging in size from the Brookesia nana chameleon (about half an inch long) to the saltwater crocodile (up to twenty feet). He made livestock, such as cattle, sheep, and goats, which provide humans with food and other resources, like wool.

Reptiles and livestock reproduce sexually when the male sperm enters and fertilizes the female egg, and the cycle of life begins all over again.

How and why did God create so many different birds, reptiles, and livestock and allow them all to be part of His re-creation plan?

Day 7: God Rested

Thus the heavens and the earth were completed in all their vast array. By the seventh day God had finished the work he had been doing; so on the seventh day he rested from all his work. Then God blessed the seventh day and made it holy, because on it he rested from all the work of creating that he had done.[19]

CREATED IN HIS IMAGE

Of all God's creation, only of mankind is it written, "...God created mankind in his own image, in the image of God he created them; male and female he created them."[20]

In the second chapter of Genesis, we are given more detail on God's process: "Then the Lord God formed a man from the dust of the ground and breathed into his nostrils the breath of life, and the man became a living being."[21]

Later, we read that no suitable helper was found for the man: "So the Lord caused the man [Adam] to fall into a deep sleep; and while he was sleeping, he took one of the man's ribs and then closed up the place with flesh. Then the Lord God made a woman from the rib he had taken out of the man, and he brought her to the man."[22]

Men and women are the pinnacle of God's creation. From the beginning, God has invited all of us to be part of His process of creating new human life—to be fruitful and multiply—by participating "in the divine nature" He ordained.

Why did God design sexual intercourse between a man and a woman to lead to new life? I am not sure, but I am thankful He did. Perhaps one day, I'll have the chance to ask Him that question in heaven.

A Special Creation Story

As I was working on this chapter about the power of creation, and ultimately about the power of our Creator, our son Stephen and his wife Caroline gave birth to our second grandson Brooks von Paris Kelly.

At birth, Brooks was twenty-one inches long and weighed eight pounds, twelve ounces. We got to meet Brooks and touch him less than an hour after he was born.

Within that first hour, we heard him cry, and he even sneezed. A few hours later, we returned to the room and spent several hours with Brooks and his parents. We held him and hugged him, and he even opened his eyes, seeming to stare right at me.

What a miracle! Just a few hours earlier, he was in his mother's womb, surrounded by amniotic fluid and sustained by his mother's blood. To think that nine months earlier, one of millions of sperm met and fertilized an egg, becoming an embryo. And then, nine months later, Brooks was welcomed into the world as a healthy baby with ten fingers, ten toes, a beautiful nose, eyes, ears, and even some hair on his head. A true creation miracle, as every life is truly a creation miracle!

And created in the image of God? I don't fully understand what that means, but I know it is awesome.

I can relate to King David's words, penned thousands of years ago in one of his Psalms, "For you [God] created my inmost being; you knit me together in my mother's womb. I praise you because I am fearfully and wonderfully made..."[23]

When you consider that the current world population is 8.1 billion people from nearly 1,500 different nationalities and ethnic groups living in one of 195 recognized countries around the world, it's truly mind-boggling.

Each year, approximately 60 million people die, and 140 million babies are born (that's four births every second of every day). And the Scriptures say God loves and knows every person by name.

How does God do that?

CREATORS AS WELL

Not all of us are called to be parents or participate in the process of helping create new life, but we are all made in the image of God and thus are creators in different ways.

At times, you may feel unproductive and hardly a part of God's creation plan. But you must remember that He has gifted you in unique ways—not only to bless and serve others but to create blessings for others as well. Even a simple word of encouragement, a written note, or a quiet gesture of kindness is uniquely created for that specific time, place, and scenario. And some of us are called to be part of creating a new business, art, music, or even a book.

I am still struggling to embrace the fact that I'm an author. Rarely do I see myself as the creative type; yet with God's inspiration, I wrote a second book in 2023 called *Influence and The Creator's Game: My Story and Stories of Family, Faith and Lacrosse.*

"Influence" represents the Gospel, or the Good News of God's love, grace, and mercy available to each of us. Some also say it is the one-word definition of the Fellowship of Christian Athletes (FCA).

"The Creator's Game," known today as lacrosse, was played by Native Americans going back to at least the 1600s. They played it to settle conflicts and prepare their youth for battle, with the ultimate goal of pleasing their Creator. They played lacrosse with passion, freedom, and creativity. The book captures my story of how I came to know the Creator through the Creator's game, lacrosse, and how many others have as well.

More significantly, God gives some people the vision and passion to create things like new medicines or technologies to save lives, cars to drive across the country, planes to fly around the world, or rockets to land on the moon and return to Earth safely.

How and why did God create us to *Go* and be creators as well?

God's creation is truly amazing and miraculous, and we are so blessed as humans to be created in His image and empowered by Him to *love* and *go* and help create amazing things, too.

What is God calling you to create?

SUGGESTED PRAYER

Dear God,

Your creation is truly amazing and miraculous. Thank You for allowing me to enjoy Your creation, even though I don't fully understand how or why You made it the way You did. Thank You for creating me in Your image. Please empower me to use the gifts You have given me to help create in ways that honor You and bless and serve others.

In Jesus' name. Amen.

The Power of Creation

TRUTH #11:

**God created the universe, and He created each of us
in His image, to be creators as well.**

QUESTIONS FOR REFLECTION

1. Do you believe God, or a higher power, created the world and life as we understand it? If so, how?

2. Do you think God created the heavens and the earth, and all that dwells within them, in six, twenty-four-hour days as we understand time, or over a longer period of time? (Consider the scripture: "...With the Lord a day is like a thousand years, and a thousand years are like a day.")

3. How does believing God created each of us in His image affect the way we live and view ourselves and life?

4. When you think of the questions, "How did God do that?" and "Why did God do that?," what aspect of creation comes to mind?

5. In your opinion, what are some of the most miraculous ways God allows His creation to be a part of creation and re-creation?

6. Do you believe God created each of us to be creators as well? What are some examples of human involvement in creation that amaze you? What is God calling you to create?

The Power of Perseverance

TRUTH #12:

**Perseverance in enduring and overcoming hardships
is key to success here on Earth and essential to refining your faith,
shaping your character, and strengthening your relationship with God.**

*"Consider it pure joy, my brothers and sisters, whenever you face trials
of many kinds, because you know that the testing of your faith produces
perseverance. Let perseverance finish its work so that you may be mature
and complete, not lacking in anything."*[1]

James*

L ife is full of difficulties, delays, and discouragement. Perseverance is the continued effort to achieve something despite those challenges, failures, or opposition.

As a former high school and college athlete, I experienced and can relate to others' stories of dealing with injuries, limited playing time, and various failures and losses.

One thing I learned as a competitive athlete and later as a decades-long coach is that winning is more fun than losing, getting playing time is more fun than sitting on the bench, and injuries and setbacks can be exceedingly difficult to deal with and endure. One of the keys to persevering as an athlete, coach, or anyone, for that matter, is perspective. The legendary baseball player Babe Ruth once said, "Every strikeout brings me closer to my next home run." For many years, Ruth held the major league career record for

---

* Some theologians refer to the author of the book of James in the Bible as "James the Just" and others refer to him as James, the half-brother or cousin of Jesus.

strikeouts, having struck out more than 1,300 times. However, he also held the record for most home runs in a career, with more than 700. Ruth knew he had to persevere through many strikeouts or failures to achieve that success. At the end of his career, Ruth noted, "It's hard to beat a person who never gives up."

I also think about Michael Jordan who many argue is the greatest basketball player of all time. In college, he led the University of North Carolina Tar Heels to a National Championship. As a pro, he led the Chicago Bulls to six NBA Championships and won six NBA Finals MVP awards. He once said, "I've missed more than 9,000 shots in my [NBA] career. I've lost almost 300 games. Twenty-six times I've been trusted to take the game-winning shot and missed. I've failed over and over in my life. And that is why I succeed."[2] Perseverance is not quitting because of failure but showing up again and again, overcoming in spite of failure and obstacles.

World War II hero and British Prime Minister Winston Churchill is often credited for saying, "Success is not final, failure is not fatal; it's the courage to continue that counts." That is true wisdom and perspective. Perseverance is about continuing despite failure.

The great American inventor Thomas Edison famously failed 999 times in his efforts to make a working light bulb. As myth has it, he was successful on his 1,000[th] attempt, creating an electric light bulb that would change the world forever. When asked about his failures, he is said to have remarked, "I have not failed at all. I have just found 999 ways that won't work."

Perspective and perseverance!

Edison, considered a genius for his hundreds of inventions and patents, said, "Genius is 1 percent inspiration and 99 percent perspiration.[3] Similarly, it's believed that he said, "It's not that I am so smart, it's just that I stay with problems longer. Many of life's failures are people who did not realize how close they were to success when they gave up."

Perseverance is about overcoming obstacles, failures, roadblocks, and difficulties.

I like the way the Apostle Paul wrote about perseverance in his letter to the young church in Galatia: "Let us not become weary in doing good, for at the proper time we will reap a harvest if we do not give up."[4]

Sometimes, when we give our best effort and try to do what is right, we don't see immediate results. The challenge is not to grow tired of doing the right things for the right reasons.

When talking about perseverance stories and examples, you can't leave out Abraham Lincoln. Born into poverty in a log cabin in Kentucky in 1809, Lincoln had to educate himself. His early life was marked by failure and disappointment.

Lincoln failed at business in 1831 and was defeated in his first run for political office in 1832. He failed again at business in 1833, and in 1835, his fiancée died. In 1836, he suffered a nervous breakdown. He lost his run for Congress in 1843 and again in 1848. He lost his run for Senate in 1855, his run for Vice President in 1856, and another run for Senate in 1859. Finally, in 1860, Lincoln was elected the sixteenth President of the United States.

His leadership and presidency would lead to the abolition of slavery and forever change the course of American history. The difference between his success and his many failures was perseverance.

Perseverance has the power to change the world.

TESTING PRODUCES PERSEVERANCE

A challenging verse in the Bible says, "Consider it pure joy, my brothers and sisters, whenever you face trials of many kinds, because you know that the testing of your faith produces perseverance. Let perseverance finish its work so that you may be mature and complete, not lacking anything."[5]

We are encouraged to embrace joy as we face various trials and hardships, knowing that the testing of our faith will ultimately produce perseverance and character, so that we can become mature, complete, and not lacking anything. Is that really true? Sounds very challenging to me. I know no one who has lived out this scripture better than my friends O.J. and Chanda Brigance. O.J. overcame many challenges and setbacks to become a college football player at Rice University, then a professional Canadian League Football player, and eventually an NFL Super Bowl Champion. As a special teams player with the Baltimore Ravens, O.J. made the first tackle in the 2001 Super Bowl XXXV game, which the Ravens won 34-7, defeating the New York Giants.

After retiring from professional football in 2002, O.J. joined the Baltimore Ravens as a senior advisor for player development. In 2007, O.J. went to see Ravens head coach Brian Billick. As he entered the office, Coach Billick, focused on preparing for the next Ravens game, did not lift his eyes from his desk. Without looking up, he said, "What's up, Juice [O.J.'s nickname]?"

O.J. replied, "Coach, I wanted to tell you about an amazing opportunity I've been blessed with. An opportunity that is going to change my life forever."

Coach Billick, still with his eyes down on his work, replied, "What, did another team offer you a better job? I don't really have time for this now, O.J."

O.J. then said, "No, Coach. No new team. No new job. I've been blessed with an opportunity far greater than that." He took a deep breath. "Coach, I have been diagnosed with ALS, or amyotrophic lateral sclerosis, also known as Lou Gehrig's Disease, and I wanted you to hear it first, directly from me."

Immediately, Coach Billick got up from behind his desk, looked O.J. in the eyes, hugged him, and expressed his sincere concern. He knew ALS is a rare, terminal disorder that ultimately results in complete paralysis, the loss of the ability to speak, eat, and eventually breathe on one's own. Most people live less than three years after an ALS diagnosis.

O.J., his wife Chanda, and their family had time to process their new reality before he shared the news with Coach Billick and the owner of the Ravens, Steve Bisciotti, who were both very supportive.

Although O.J. and Chanda were upset and disappointed, they decided to look at this challenge as a test and ultimately a blessing from God. They actually chose to embrace this diagnosis as an opportunity from God to grow in their relationship with Him and to be a light and encouragement to others dealing with a difficult diagnosis.

Doctors gave O.J. a maximum of three to five years to live. As of this writing, O.J. has lived with ALS for eighteen years.

Although he is completely paralyzed and unable to speak on his own, he still works in player development with the Ravens. Many players come to his office to talk with him.

Despite not being able to speak for many years now, O.J. has learned to use a special computer that allows him to spell out words and sentences with his eyes, which the computer then translates into speech. Using his eyes, he can also send and respond to emails, text messages, and even prepare speeches that his computer voice delivers.

In 2008, a year after his diagnosis, O.J. and Chanda created the Brigance Brigade Foundation, which my dad and I were blessed to be founding board members of. The foundation supports and encourages people living with ALS and their families by providing resources like electric wheelchairs, special computers, and handicapped accessible vans. Over the years, the Foundation has helped hundreds of families throughout the Mid-Atlantic region and beyond.

In 2013, O.J. co-wrote a book about his life called *Strength of a Champion: Finding Faith and Fortitude through Adversity.* O.J.'s perseverance and fortitude to live as a fully paralyzed man in a wheelchair have resulted in thousands of lives being blessed, strengthened, and encouraged.

Dr. Martin Luther King Jr. once said, "If you can't fly, run, if you can't run, walk; if you can't walk, crawl; but by all means keep moving."[6] O.J. and Chanda Brigance keep moving forward, helping bless and encourage many others along the way.

In 2018, the Maryland Fellowship of Christian Athletes established the O.J. Brigance Courage Award, presented each year at their annual banquet to a student-athlete or coach who exemplifies faith, focus, and fortitude by persevering and overcoming adversity in their life.

Many of O.J.'s prepared speeches, spoken through his computer, have brought inspiration, encouragement, tears, and joy to those blessed to be in attendance.

Perseverance, Character, Hope

In many ways, O.J. and Chanda have lived out the verse written by the Apostle Paul to the early church in Rome: "…we also celebrate in our tribulations, knowing that tribulation brings about perseverance; and perseverance, proven character; and proven character, hope; and hope does not disappoint…"[7]

Rick Warren reminds us, "God's ultimate goal for our life is not comfort, but character development. He wants us to grow up spiritually and become like Jesus. God is much more concerned about our character than our career, because we will take our character, not our career, into eternity. Our circumstances are temporary, but our character will last forever."[8]

Perseverance leads to character, and character to hope.

Television personality Hal Lindsay once said, "A person can live forty days without food, about three days without water, eight minutes without air, but only one second without hope." And bestselling author and speaker Matthew Kelly reminds us, "Hope is a good thing, maybe the best of things. Hope is the one thing people cannot live without."[9]

No one gives us greater hope than Jesus. In the book of Hebrews, we read, "…And let us run with perseverance the race marked out for us, fixing our eyes on Jesus, the pioneer and perfecter of our faith. For the joy set before him, he endured the cross, scorning its shame, and sat down at the right hand of the throne of God."[10]

PAYING THE ULTIMATE PRICE

Although we are called to run or live this life with perseverance, which can be challenging, Jesus modeled true perseverance. He followed His Father's plan to the point of death on a cross, providing us with ultimate joy and hope through the cleansing of our sin and the opportunity to have a personal relationship with God, leading to eternity in His presence.

Some of the greatest examples of perseverance, and the strongest evidence that Jesus not only lived, died on a cross, was buried, and most significantly, rose from the dead, and is who He claims to be, is the fact that

His closest followers were willing to live their lives proclaiming that truth and die a martyr's death for it.

Most people are not willing to die for a worthy cause, but no one is willing to die for something they know to be a lie. Yet, these men, known today as the Twelve Apostles, persevered and paid the ultimate price:

- Paul was beaten and imprisoned many times and was ultimately beheaded in Rome.

- Peter was crucified upside down.

- Simon the Zealot was sawn in half.

- Matthew was killed by a sword in Ethiopia.

- James was killed by a sword and most likely beheaded by King Herod.

- Thomas was stabbed by a spear on a missionary trip to India.

- Mathias (who replaced Judas Iscariot) was stoned and then beheaded in Rome.

- Bartholomew, also known as Nathaneal, was flayed or whipped to death and beheaded.

- Andrew was crucified on an X-shaped cross in Greece after being severely whipped by seven soldiers who tied his body to the cross with cords to prolong his agony. His followers reported that he continued to preach the Gospel to his tormentors for two days until he died.

- John was boiled alive in a huge basin of oil in Rome. Miraculously, he survived and was eventually exiled to the rocky island of Patmos. There, he wrote the book of Revelation, which is the last book in the Bible.

Talk about perseverance! All they had to do to live was renounce their faith in Jesus and stop talking about Him. But they refused. Perseverance doesn't always result in worldly success or safety.

Just think how different life would be today for so many if these men had not been intentional and faithful to share God's love and truth around the world.

FIGHT, FINISH, FAITH

I marvel at real-life stories of perseverance. As a lover of sports, I am inspired by athletes who overcome failure and great challenges. As a business and community leader, I admire those who rise above obstacles to achieve success and influence. Yet, as a follower of Jesus, I am truly blown away by those in the early church who persevered and paid the ultimate price to proclaim the love and truth of God.

The Apostle Paul wrote in a letter to his young friend and mentee Timothy, "I have fought the good fight, I have finished the race, I have kept the faith. Now there is in store for me the crown of righteousness, which the Lord . . . will award to me on that day—and not only to me, but also to all who have longed for his appearing."[11] Paul's reward for persevering would be an eternal one—one he would receive after his death, and that would last forever.

When Paul was beaten, imprisoned, and ultimately beheaded in Rome for his faith in Jesus, the result of his perseverance may have appeared fruitless and a waste. Yet, his perseverance resulted in an eternal crown or reward in heaven and an impact on billions of people over the millennia—generations who would be transformed and saved by the words God wrote through him.

Sometimes, you don't see, experience, or realize the fruit of your perseverance on this side of eternity. The challenge, whether as an individual, a family, a team, or a business, is not to quit and to diligently continue to fight the good fight, finish the race, and keep the faith.

Jesus is the greatest example of perseverance, character, hope, and love. He wants to help you and me grow in each of these areas. Jesus is love, and the Scriptures remind us, "It always protects, always trusts, always hopes, and always perseveres."[12]

As we come down the homestretch of this chapter and book, there are a few questions worth considering in light of Jesus' love and perseverance:

- Are you committed to growing in your relationship with God?
- Do you want to persevere in fulfilling your God given potential and purpose in life?

- Will you embrace and apply the powerful truths you have read and learned about in this book?

- Are you ready to love and go with purpose and power?

God wants to help you and me persevere in fighting the good fight, finishing the race strong, and both gaining and keeping the faith. And His Word reminds us that it is "...him who is able to do immeasurably more than all we can ask or imagine, according to his power that is at work within us . . . throughout all generations, for ever and ever."[13]

The decision to *love* and *go* is yours. Are you ready to make it? If so, let's *Go!*

SUGGESTED PRAYER

Dear God,

I desire to fully trust You and ask for Your help to overcome and persevere through life's challenges. Thank You for the examples of those who have persevered to accomplish great things, and for those who persevered and paid the ultimate price to share Your love and truth with others. Most importantly, thank You, Jesus, for persevering—even to the point of being crucified, dying on a cross, and rising from the dead—so that my sins could be forgiven. By Your grace, may I love and go with perseverance, fighting the good fight, finishing the race, and gaining and keeping the faith. All for Your glory!

In Jesus' name. Amen.

CHAPTER 12

The Power of Perseverance

TRUTH #12:

**Perseverance in enduring and overcoming hardships
is key to success here on Earth and essential to refining your faith,
shaping your character, and strengthening your relationship with God.**

QUESTIONS FOR REFLECTION

1. When you think of perseverance, who comes to mind? In this chapter, which example(s) of human perseverance stood out to you and why?

2. What do you think about Dr. Martin Luther King Jr.'s quote, "If you can't fly, then run, if you can't run, then walk, if you can't walk, then crawl, but whatever you do, you have to keep moving forward"?

3. What is something you have had to persevere through (e.g., a class, injury, job, marriage, health condition, etc.)? What is one thing you believe God is leading you to persevere through at this time?

4. Do you believe perseverance produces character? Do you agree with Rick Warren's quote, "God's ultimate goal for our life is not comfort, but character development," and that "our character will last forever"? Why or why not?

5. When you consider Jesus' life, death, and resurrection, do you think about perseverance, character, hope, and/or love? Why?

6. What strikes you about the way Jesus' Twelve Apostles lived and died?

CONCLUSION

The great UCLA basketball coach, John Wooden, once said, "It's what you learn after you know everything, that counts."

I am thankful for all I have learned over my first sixty physical and forty spiritual years (60/40); yet, I know there is so much more God wants me to learn, understand, and better apply to my life.

I have heard it said that "leaders are learners" and "leaders are readers."

I hope the twelve powerful truths you have read about in this book prove to be a valuable source of learning, practical inspiration, and blessing as you contemplate how you can most effectively *love* and *go* and fulfill your unique God-given potential and purpose in life.

Please note that in the Addendum, I share some relevant information on how to enter into a personal, real, life-changing relationship with God, as well as help others do the same.

If you have questions or want to connect about anything you have read, feel free to email me at fxkelly@kellybenefits.com.

Now it's time to *Love & Go!*

A Personal Invitation

We all like to be included or invited to special events, and it's always nice when someone remembers and calls us by name.

In the Gospel of Matthew, Jesus tells the story of a king who prepared an incredible wedding celebration for his son. After sending out the invitations, the king was deeply hurt by those who didn't respond or chose not to attend. They made all kinds of excuses and even harassed the king's servants who delivered the invitations.[1]

Gayle and I remember sending out wedding invitations for our two oldest sons' weddings. We worked so hard on the guest list and couldn't invite everyone we wanted, so it was especially hurtful and frustrating when some people didn't even respond. It was even more disappointing when others decided not to come at the last minute. We had prepared an amazing celebration, and a number of people blew off the invitation.

That's how the king felt, so he opened up the wedding party to everyone, including people off the street. This story is a parable illustrating the Kingdom of Heaven and how God has invited all of us to respond to His invitation to enter into a relationship with Him through His Son, Jesus Christ. By saying yes to this invitation, we can experience the peace, joy, and blessings of a personal relationship with Him and, one day, enter the Kingdom of Heaven.

In the Gospel of Luke, we read another story where Jesus was walking through the town of Jericho on His way to Jerusalem. The crowds were so big that a man named Zacchaeus, who was short in stature, ran ahead and climbed a sycamore tree to see Jesus as He passed by. "When Jesus reached the spot, he looked up and said to him, 'Zacchaeus, come down immediately. I must stay at your house today.' So he came down at once and welcomed him gladly. All the people saw this began to mutter, 'He has gone to be the guest of a sinner.'"[2]

How did Jesus know Zacchaeus' name when He had never met or heard of him before? The truth is, Jesus knows everyone by name, and He sincerely wants a relationship with sinners like you and me. Zacchaeus was well known as a corrupt tax collector and was hated by everyone, but Jesus still called him by name and spent time with him.

Jesus understood—and still understands—the power of a name, the power of an invitation, and the power of grace.

When it comes to the power of a name, we read in Paul's letter to the Philippians that "...God highly exalted Him, and bestowed on Him the name which is above every name, so that at the name of Jesus every knee will bow... and that every tongue will confess that Jesus Christ is Lord..."[3]

Jesus knows your name—He truly does—and He invites you to have a relationship with Him and to come to the amazing wedding feast and banquet His Father has prepared for you and for all He calls to experience the abundant life He promises.

God also gives us the blessing of inviting our family and friends into a relationship with Him and to His wedding feast as well.

You don't want to ignore or say no to this invitation, as it has lifelong and eternal implications. This is one relationship and celebration you do not want to miss.

See THE FOUR on the next page as a helpful visual and summary.

THE FOUR

As you have read this book about powerful truths, you may have a question or two about what you really need to know to say yes to God's invitation and begin your own personal, eternal relationship with Him. Or you may want a practical way to help share God's love and truth with others so they can enter into and grow in a personal relationship with God.

A simple summary of the Gospel that has helped me and others is commonly referred to as "The Four" and includes:

God's Position
God is perfect, holy, loving, and kind. He made you and loves you, and He wants you to experience His love and discover His purpose for your life through a personal relationship with Him.
(Genesis 1:27; Matthew 5:48; John 3:16)

Our Condition
We are all sinners who are broken and fall short of God's standard of perfection, and our sin separates or divides us from Him.
(Romans 3:23; Romans 6:23; Isaiah 59:2)

God's Provision
God, in the person of Jesus Christ, took the initiative to redeem or save us. Through His life, death on the cross, shed blood, and resurrection from the dead, Jesus offers cleansing for our sins. Because of God's provision, we can experience God's love, discover our purpose for life, and after death, spend eternity in perfect peace in His presence.
(1 Peter 3:18; 1 John 4:10)

Our Decision
Will you acknowledge God's position of perfection, holiness, and love? Will you repent and admit your condition as a sinner—broken, separated, and divided from God? Will you recognize God's provision and profess with your mouth that Jesus is Lord, and that God raised Him from the dead? Will you believe, receive, and follow Jesus as your Savior and Lord? The decision is yours.
(Romans 10:9-13; John 1:12; 1 John 5:11-12)

In the book of Revelation, the Apostle John records the words of Jesus when he writes, "Here I am! I stand at the door and knock. If anyone hears my voice and opens the door, I will come in and eat with that person, and they with me."[4]

Is Jesus knocking on the door of your heart? Are you ready to open that door and invite Jesus into your life? Are you ready to respond yes to God's invitation?

You can begin your relationship with God by faith through prayer. The actual words of your prayer are not as important as your heart, but the words/prayer below may be helpful.

SUGGESTED PRAYER

Dear God,

♥ *This day, I pray and acknowledge that You are perfect, holy, loving, and kind. You are all-powerful, all-knowing, and everywhere present, and I thank You for loving me and wanting me to experience abundant life in You.*

÷ *I realize I have sinned and that my sin divides, or separates, me from You and Your best for me. I've made many mistakes doing things my way, and I am sorry.*

✝ *Jesus, thank You for dying on the cross and rising from the dead three days later as a provision for my sins and the sins of the world.*

❓ *I have decided to turn from my sin, trust You, and ask You to come into my heart/life and help me become the person You created and desire me to be. I surrender my life to You and acknowledge that You are my Savior and Lord, and I look forward to growing in my relationship with You.*

💚 *Thank You for loving and forgiving me, coming into my heart, empowering me to love and go, and giving me the gift of eternal life. In Jesus' name, Amen.*

ACKNOWLEDGEMENTS

I have always loved team sports, especially football and lacrosse, and can tell you that writing a book takes a true team effort. I want to thank and acknowledge all of my teammates who helped make the vision of this book a reality, including:

Everyone who has poured truth into my life over the years.

My wife Gayle, who prayed for, supported, and encouraged me through many early morning and late-night writing and editing sessions.

My assistant Kenzie Turpin for her amazing typing, editing, and organizational skills.

Jen Jardell and Danielle Ripley-Burgess for their invaluable content and copy editing, corrections, and suggestions.

All the People of Kelly Benefits who reviewed content and gave valuable feedback, including Heather Kness, who helped with the cover design, and Amanda Merrey, who helped review and inform our accurate use of Scripture.

Jennifer Kozak, who designed the layout and refined the cover with creative skill and brilliance.

All of my friends and associates who read all or parts of my early drafts and gave insightful feedback, including Bill Tamulonis, Steve Harrison, Chuck Knudsen, Shaun Smithson, Jay McCumber, Paul MacMillan, Fr. Michael White, Tom Corcoran, Jen Silberzahn, Tony Keryakos, Mike Donohue Jr., Shawna Garliss, Mark Warren, and my daughter Jackie Lee Kelly. I didn't take or use every bit of advice; so, if this book is not great, only I am to blame.

Kathryn Gordon and the Gordon Publishing team, and especially Dave Sheets and Believers Book Services.

The dozens of people who have encouraged, prayed for, and cheered me on during this process. You know who you are, and I appreciate you.

My Creator and Heavenly Father, His Son Jesus, and the Holy Spirit for loving me, saving me, empowering me, and choosing to reveal truth to and through me.

Thank you, Team! I am grateful for the many ways you have served me in writing and producing this book. I am honored to call you teammates.

NOTES

CHAPTER 1

1 2 Timothy 3:16-17

2 Josh McDowell, *Evidence That Demands a Verdict, rev. ed.* (Nashville, TN: Thomas Nelson, 1979).

3 Rick Warren, "The Whole Bible Points to Jesus," Daily Hope devotional, iDisciple, 2023.

4 Rick Warren, "You Can Trust the Bible," Daily Hope devotional, iDisciple, 2023.

5 Ramm, Bernard. *Protestant Christian Evidences* (Chicago: Moody Press, 1953).

6 John 18:38

7 Matthew 27:19, ESV

8 John 14:6

9 Matthew 7:24-27

10 John 8:31-32

11 Mark Twain, *Man Is the Only Animal that Blushes...or Needs To: The Wisdom of Mark Twain, selected by Michael Joseph* (Los Angeles: Stanyan Books; New York: Random House, 1970).

12 2 Timothy 3:16-17

13 Hebrews 4:12, NASB

14 Psalm 119:105

15 Isaiah 40:8

16 Luke 21:33

17 Rick Warren, "What's Your Final Authority?" Daily Hope with Rick Warren (devotional), April 9, 2021, Lightsource.

CHAPTER 2

1 Psalm 22:3, KJV (paraphrased)

2 Acts 16:23-34

3 Psalm 22:3

4 1 Thessalonians 5:16-18

CHAPTER 3

1 James 5:16b

2 Luke 11:1

3 Matthew 6:9-13, Book of Common Prayer

4 Fr. Michael White and Tom Corcoran, *Rebuilt Faith: A Handbook for Skeptical Catholics* (Notre Dame, IN: Ave Maria Press, 2023).

5 Luke 11:4, Book of Common Prayer

6 Romans 3:23

7 Romans 6:23

8 James 5:16

9 1 John 1:9

10 Matthew 6:14-15

11 Psalm 136:1

12 1 Thessalonians 5:16-18

13 Philippians 4:6-7

14 Matthew 6:13, Book of Common Prayer

15 John 16:24

16 Rick Warren, "Relax! God Is Working for Your Good," Daily Hope with Rick Warren (devotional), September 25, 2024, PastorRick.com.

17 Isaiah 55:9

18 Luke 18:1

19 1 Kings 19:12

20 1 Kings 19:11-13

21 Mark 1:35

22 Mark 6:31

23 Henri J. M. Nouwen, *The Way of the Heart: Desert Spirituality and Contemporary Ministry* (New York: Harper & Row, 1981).

24 Psalm 46:10

25 1 John 1:9

26 Henry T. Blackaby and Claude V. King, *Experiencing God: Knowing and Doing the Will of God* (Nashville, TN: Broadman & Holman Publishers, 1994).

27 Jeff Caliguire and Mindy Caliguire, *Write for Your Soul: The Whys and Hows of Journaling* (Colorado Springs, CO: Soul Care Communications, LLC), 1999.

28 Numbers 6:24-26

29 Proverbs 3:3-4, paraphrased

30 Luke 2:52

31 Psalm 91:11

32 Galatians 5:22-23, NASB

33 John 16:33

34 Luke 12:6-7, NKJV

35 Rick Warren, "Pray About Everything," Daily Hope with Rick Warren (devotional), October 2, 2021, Crosswalk.

36 Ephesians 6:12

37 Matthew 26:40-41, ESV

38 James 5:16b

39 Matthew 18:20

CHAPTER 4

1 Acts 1:8

2 Galatians 5:22-23, NASB

3 Acts 1:8

4 Acts 2:3

5 Ephesians 5:18

6 Bill Bright, The Holy Spirit: *The Key to Supernatural Living* (San Bernardino, CA: Campus Crusade for Christ International, 1986).

7 Galatians 5:22-23, NASB

8 John 10:10, NASB

9 1 John 1:9

10 Ephesians 5:18

CHAPTER 5

1 Romans 10:17, NKJV

2 Matthew 17:20

3 Rick Warren, "Choose Faith over Fear," Daily Hope with Rick Warren (devotional), September 21, 2020, Lightsource.

4 Hebrews 11:6

5 Mark 9:17-24, 29, NKJV (paraphrased)

6 Ephesians 2:8-9

7 Rick Warren, Daily Hope Devotional Series

8 2 Timothy 1:7, NKJV

9 1 John 4:18, ESV

10 Lloyd John Ogilvie, *Facing the Future Without Fear: Prescriptions for Courageous Living in the New Millennium* (Ann Arbor, MI: Vine Books, 1999).

11 Psalm 56:3-4

12 Proverbs 3:5-6, NKJV

13 Jeremiah 29:11

14 Isaiah 55:8-9

15 James 2:20, NKJV

16 Romans 10:17, NKJV

CHAPTER 6

1 James 1:5

2 1 Kings 3:5-13

3 James 1:5

4 Rick Warren, "Fill Your Mind with Truth, Not Poison," Daily Hope with Rick Warren (devotional), September 4, 2016, Crosswalk.

5 Psalm 127:2b

6 Rick Warren, "Where to Find Real Wisdom," Daily Hope with Rick Warren (devotional), January 15, 2021, Crosswalk.

7 Dan Britton and Jimmy Page, *Wisdom Walks: 40 Life Principles for a Significant & Meaningful Journey, foreword by Kevin Leman* (Minneapolis, MN: BroadStreet Publishing Group, 2014).

8 Rick Warren, *The Purpose Driven Life: What on Earth Am I Here For?* (Grand Rapids, MI: Zondervan, 2012).

9 Proverbs 13:20, ESV

10 Proverbs 1:7

11 Matthew 20:16

12 2 Corinthians 12:9-10

13 Romans 12:1

14 Rick Warren, "Let Go, and Know God Is in Control," Daily Hope with Rick Warren (devotional), May 6, 2025, PastorRick.com.

15 Rick Warren, *The Purpose Driven Life: What on Earth Am I Here For?* (Grand Rapids, MI: Zondervan, 2012), 287.

16 Reinhold Niebuhr, *The Essential Reinhold Niebuhr: Selected Essays and Addresses, ed. Robert McAfee Brown* (New Haven, CT: Yale University Press, 1986).

[17] Isaiah 55:8-9

[18] Matthew 7:1-2

[19] Rick Warren, "Wise People Choose Mercy," Daily Hope with Rick Warren (devotional), July 24, 2024, Crosswalk.

[20] Romans 12:17, 21

[21] Dr. Martin Luther King Jr., *"Loving Your Enemies," in Strength to Love* (New York: Harper & Row, 1963).

[22] John 8:12

[23] Ephesians 5:18

[24] Ephesians 4:29

[25] Proverbs 18:21

[26] James 1:19

[27] Psalm 103:8

[28] Matthew 11:28

[29] Matthew 4:19, NASB

[30] Proverbs 3:5-6, NASB

[31] Psalm 37:4, NASB

CHAPTER 7

[1] Romans 8:28

[2] Matthew 6:19-20, NASB

[3] C. T. Studd, *"Only One Life," in Quaint Rhymes for the Battlefield* (London: James Clarke & Co., 1914).

[4] Jim Elliot, journal entry, October 28, 1949, quoted in Elisabeth Elliot, *Shadow of the Almighty: The Life and Testament of Jim Elliot* (New York: Harper & Row, 1958).

[5] Acts 1:8, NASB 1995

[6] Colossians 3:23-24b

[7] Isaiah 55:8-9

[8] Romans 8:28

[9] Mark 12:28-31

[10] Matthew 28:19-20

[11] Rick Warren, *The Purpose Driven Life: What on Earth Am I Here For?* (Grand Rapids, MI: Zondervan, 2002).

[12] Jeremiah 1:5, MSG

[13] Psalm 139:13-14

[14] Ephesians 2:10

[15] Rick Warren, "This Christmas, Get to Know Your Savior," Daily Hope with Rick Warren (devotional), December 16, 2023, Lightsource.

[16] Rick Warren, *The Purpose Driven Life: What on Earth Am I Here For?* (Grand Rapids, MI: Zondervan, 2002).

[17] Proverbs 19:21

CHAPTER 8

[1] Luke 6:38

[2] Luke 6:38

[3] Luke 6:38

[4] Acts 20:35

[5] Matthew 6:21

[6] Proverbs 3:9-10

[7] Rick Warren, "Tithe for the Past, Present, and Future," Daily Hope with Rick Warren (devotional), January 13, 2021, Oneplace.com.

[8] Malachi 3:10

[9] Psalm 50:10-11

[10] 2 Corinthians 9:7

[11] Matthew 6:19-20, NASB

[12] Randy Alcorn, *The Treasure Principle: Discovering the Secret of Joyful Giving* (Colorado Springs, CO: Multnomah Publishers, 2001).

[13] Matthew 6:3-4

[14] Mark 12:41-44

[15] Psalm 90:12

[16] Psalm 90:10

[17] Psalm 139:16

[18] Ephesians 5:15-16a, NASB 1995

[19] Matthew 25:14-30

[20] 1 Peter 3:15

[21] Acts 3:6-8

[22] John 14:6

[23] John 8:31-32

[24] John 1:41-42

[25] 1 Thessalonians 5:16-18

[26] Luke 17:13

[27] Luke 17:18

28 2 Corinthians 9:6

29 Proverbs 11:24-25

30 Rick Warren, "Six Reasons to Develop the Habit of Generosity," Pastors.com, n.d.

CHAPTER 9

1 Hebrews 10:24-25

2 Proverbs 14:4, ESV

3 Rick Warren, *The Purpose Driven Life: What on Earth Am I Here For?* (Grand Rapids, MI: Zondervan, 2002), 130.

4 1 Thessalonians 5:11

5 John 13:34

6 James 5:16

7 1 Thessalonians 4:18

8 Ephesians 4:32

9 Matthew 18:20

10 Rick Warren, quoted in "You Were Made for a Better Life," Angelus News, March 18, 2015.

11 Ephesians 6:1-3

12 Exodus 20:12

13 Proverbs 12:15, NASB 1995

14 Proverbs 20:15-22

15 Proverbs 17:17

16 Mark 2:1-12

17 James 5:16, NASB

18 Proverbs 27:17

19 Ecclesiastes 4:9-12

20 Ephesians 5:21-25

21 Matthew 19:5-6

22 Psalm 127:3-5

23 Deuteronomy 6:4-7

24 Ephesians 6:4

25 Proverbs 22:6, ESV, paraphrased

26 Proverbs 1:8-9

27 Mark Batterson, *Please, Sorry, Thanks: The Three Words That Change Everything* (Colorado Springs, CO: Multnomah, 2023).

CHAPTER 10

1 John 10:10, NASB 1995

2 1 Peter 5:8

3 Jon Gordon, *The Garden: A Spiritual Fable About Ways to Overcome Fear, Anxiety, and Stress* (Hoboken, NJ: John Wiley & Sons, 2020).

4 John 8:44

5 1 Corinthians 14:33

6 John 10:10

7 Ephesians 6:12

8 C. S. Lewis, *The Screwtape Letters* (New York: HarperOne, 2001).

9 Revelation 12:7-10

10 Revelation 12:4

11 Luke 10:18

12 Mark 8:38

13 Chip Ingram, *The Invisible War: What Every Believer Needs to Know about Satan, Demons, and Spiritual Warfare*, updated and expanded ed. (Grand Rapids, MI: Baker Books, 2015).

14 1 John 4:4, NASB

15 Matthew 4:1-11

16 Rick Warren, "Love Drives Out Fear," Daily Hope with Rick Warren (devotional), April 10, 2025, PastorRick.com.

17 John 8:44

18 2 Corinthians 11:14-15, NASB

19 Revelation 3:20, NASB

20 Neil T. Anderson, *The Bondage Breaker: Overcoming Negative Thoughts, Irrational Feelings, Habitual Sins*, rev. and updated ed. (Eugene, OR: Harvest House Publishers, 2019).

21 John 8:31-33

22 John 14:6

23 Matthew 9:33, NASB 1995

24 Mark 5:2-3, NASB

25 Mark 5:18-19

26 Luke 8:2, NASB

27 Ephesians 6:13-17

28 Philippians 4:7

29 Andre Ngambu, *The Blood of Jesus Christ: In Spiritual Warfare* (North Charleston, SC: CreateSpace Independent Publishing Platform, 2017).

30 Revelation 12:11, KJV

31 Exodus 12

32 John 1:29

33 James 4:7, NASB 1995

34 1 Corinthians 15:57, NASB

CHAPTER 11

1 Genesis 1:1

2 Matthew 6:26

3 Matthew 6:28-29, 31

4 Genesis 1:1

5 Psalm 33:9

6 2 Peter 3:8

7 Genesis 1:1-5

8 John 8:12

9 Genesis 1:6-8

10 "Why Is the Sky Blue?" K-12 Education – Atmosphere, National Environmental Satellite, Data, and Information Service (NESDIS), National Oceanic and Atmospheric Administration.

11 Genesis 1:9-14

12 Genesis 1:14-19

13 "The Milky Way Galaxy," OLogy: Astronomy, American Museum of Natural History.

14 Neil Armstrong, live lunar surface transmission, July 20, 1969, Apollo 11 Mission, NASA audio transcript.

15 Psalm 8:3-4

16 Psalm 147:4

17 Genesis 1:20-23

18 Genesis 1:24-28, 31

19 Genesis 2:1-3

20 Genesis 1:27

21 Genesis 2:7

22 Genesis 2:21-22

23 Psalm 139:13-14

CHAPTER 12

1 James 1:2-4

2 Nike, "Failure," television commercial featuring Michael Jordan, 30 sec.,

Wieden+Kennedy, first aired 1997.

3 Thomas A. Edison, quoted in "Famous Quotes by Thomas Edison," Thomas Edison National Historical Park.

4 Galatians 6:9

5 James 1:2-4

6 Dr. Martin Luther King Jr., "Keep Moving from This Mountain," address at Spelman College, Atlanta, GA, April 10, 1960, The Martin Luther King, Jr. Research and Education Institute, Stanford University.

7 Romans 5:3-5, NASB

8 Rick Warren, *Meditations on the Purpose-Driven Life* (Grand Rapids, MI: Zondervan, 2003).

9 Matthew Kelly, *Rediscovering Catholicism: Journeying Toward Our Spiritual North Star* (Beacon Pub., 2002).

10 Hebrews 12:1-2

11 2 Timothy 4:7-8

12 1 Corinthians 13:7

13 Ephesians 3:20-21

ADDENDUM

1 Matthew 22:1-14

2 Luke 19:5-7

3 Philippians 2:9-11, NASB

4 Revelation 3:20

ABOUT THE AUTHOR

Frank Kelly III is CEO of Kelly Benefits, a family business he leads with his three brothers.

A 1986 graduate of Cornell University, Frank was recognized as a Red Key Scholar-Athlete, played football, and captained the lacrosse team. His interest in lacrosse continued after college, playing several seasons of professional indoor lacrosse, many years of high-level field lacrosse, and coaching youth and high school sports for decades.

Frank has served on boards and in leadership roles for many nonprofit organizations and has been inducted into the Halls of Fame of his high school (Calvert Hall), business/industry (Maryland Association of Health Underwriters) and lacrosse community (US Lacrosse Greater Baltimore Chapter) as well as the Fellowship of Christian Athletes Hall of Champions. Frank is also the author of *Look & See* and *Influence and The Creator's Game: My Story and Stories of Family, Faith and Lacrosse.*

Frank and his wife, Gayle, are grateful parents of four children, two beautiful daughters-in-law, and three precious grandsons. They live in Lutherville, Maryland.

Other Books by Frank Kelly III

FrankKellyIII.com LoveAndGo.com